UNDERSTANDING AND USING

ENGLISH GRAMMAR

Second Edition

TEACHER'S GUIDE
Volume A

UNDERSTANDING AND USING

ENGLISH GRAMMAR

Second Edition

TEACHER'S GUIDE
Volume A

Barbara F. Matthies
Betty Schrampfer Azar

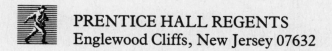

PRENTICE HALL REGENTS
Englewood Cliffs, New Jersey 07632

Publisher: Tina B. Carver
Managing editor, production: Sylvia Moore
Editorial/production supervision: Janet Johnston
Interior design: Ros Herion Freese
Cover design: Joel Mitnick Design
Manufacturing buyers: Ray Keating, Lori Bulwin

© 1991 by Prentice-Hall, Inc.
A Division of Simon & Schuster
Englewood Cliffs, New Jersey 07632

Printed in the United States of America

10 9 8 7 6 5 4 3

ISBN 0-13-943994-3

Prentice-Hall International (UK) Limited, *London*
Prentice-Hall of Australia Pty. Limited, *Sydney*
Prentice-Hall Canada Inc., *Toronto*
Prentice-Hall Hispanoamericana, S.A., *Mexico*
Prentice-Hall of India Private Limited, *New Delhi*
Prentice-Hall of Japan, Inc., *Tokyo*
Simon & Schuster Asia Pte. Ltd., *Singapore*
Editora Prentice-Hall do Brasil, Ltda., *Rio de Janeiro*

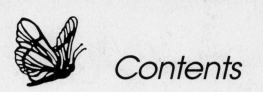

Contents

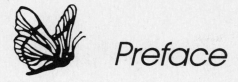

Preface

This *Teacher's Guide* is intended as a practical aid to teachers. You can turn to it for notes on the content of a unit and how to approach the exercises, for suggestions for classroom activities, and for answers to the exercises in the main text and to the Guided Study practices in the workbooks.

General teaching information can be found in the introduction. It includes:

- the rationale and general aims of *Understanding and Using English Grammar*
- classroom techniques for presenting charts and using exercises
- suggestions on the use of the workbook in connection with the main text
- comments on differences between American and British English
- a key to the pronunciation symbols used in this *Guide*

The rest of the *Guide* contains notes on charts and exercises.

The notes about the charts may include:

- suggestions for presenting the information to students
- points to emphasize
- common problems to anticipate
- assumptions underlying the contents
- additional background notes on grammar and usage

The notes that accompany the exercises may include:

- the focus of the exercise
- suggested techniques as outlined in the introduction
- possible specialized techniques for particular exercises
- points to emphasize
- problems to anticipate
- assumptions
- answers
- expansion activities
- item notes on cultural content, vocabulary, and idiomatic usage. (Some of these item notes are specifically intended to aid any teachers who are non-native speakers of English.)

This *Teacher's Guide* is divided into two volumes. *Volume A* contains the introduction and the notes and answers for Chapters 1 through 4 and Appendix 1. *Volume B* contains the notes and answers for Chapters 5 through 10.

Introduction

General Aims of *Understanding and Using English Grammar*

The principal aim of *Understanding and Using English Grammar* is, simply put, to provide review and reinforcement of basic English structures and, upon this foundation, to enable the students to expand their performance repertoire in all skill areas. The text seeks to apprise English language students of certain grammatical features of high frequency and utility in English. As learners become aware of these structures, they begin to see and hear them more easily. This can lead, in turn, to more success in using the structures naturally and appropriately in their own speaking and writing, especially if they are provided with numerous practice opportunities. The exercises provide practice in listening, speaking, reading, and writing skills, since grammar underlies all of them.

The text depends upon a partnership with a teacher, for the teacher animates and directs the students' language-learning experiences. In practical terms, the aim of the text is to support teachers by providing a substantial base of material to be used creatively according to their needs and preferences.

Classroom Techniques

Following are some techniques that have proven useful. *Suggestions for Presenting the Grammar Charts* are discussed first. Next are some notes on *Degrees of Teacher and Student Involvement.* Then *Techniques for Exercise Types* are outlined.

Suggestions for Presenting the Grammar Charts

A chart is a concise visual presentation of the structures to be covered in one section of a chapter. Some charts may require particular methods of presentation, but generally any of the following techniques can be used.

Technique #1: Use the examples in the chart and your own examples to explain the grammar in your own words, and answer any questions about the chart. Elicit other examples of the target structure from the learners. Then go to the accompanying exercise immediately following the chart.

Technique #2: Elicit oral examples from the students before they look at the chart in the textbook. To elicit examples from the students, ask leading questions whose answers will include the target structure. (For example, for the present progressive, ask: "What are you doing right now?") You may want to write the elicited answers on the chalkboard and relate them to the examples in the chart. Then proceed to the exercises.

Technique #3: Assign the chart and accompanying exercise(s) for out-of-class study. In class the next day, ask for and answer any questions about the chart, and then immediately proceed to the exercises. (With advanced students, you might not need to deal thoroughly in class with every chart and exercise. With intermediate students, it is usually advisable to clarify charts and do most of the exercises.)

Technique #4: Lead the students through the accompanying exercise prior to discussing the chart. Use the material in the exercise to discuss the focus of the chart as you go along. At the end of the exercise, call attention to the examples in the chart and summarize what was discussed during the exercise.

Technique #5: Before presenting the chart in class, give the students a short written quiz on its content. Have the students correct their own papers as you review the answers. The quiz should not be given a score; it is a learning tool, not an examination. Use the items from the quiz as examples for discussing the grammar in the chart.

Presentation techniques often depend upon the content of the chart, the level of the class, and the students' learning styles. Not all students react to the charts in the same ways. Some students need the security of thoroughly understanding a chart before trying to use the structure. Others like to experiment more freely with using new structures; they refer to the charts only incidentally, if at all. Given these differing learning strategies, you should vary your presentation techniques and not expect students to "learn" or memorize the charts. The charts are just a starting point for class discussion and a point of reference.

Demonstration can be very helpful to explain the meaning of structures. You and the students can act out situations that demonstrate the target structure. Of course, not all grammar lends itself to this technique. For example, the present progressive can easily be demonstrated ("I *am writing* on the board right now."). However, the use of gerunds as the objects of prepositions ("instead *of writing*" or "thank you *for writing*") is not especially well suited to demonstration techniques.

In discussing the target structure of a chart, use the chalkboard whenever possible. Not all students have adequate listening skills for "teacher talk," and not all students can visualize and understand the various relationships within, between, and among structures. Draw boxes and circles and arrows to illustrate connections between the elements of a structure.

The students need to understand the terminology, but shouldn't be required or expected to give detailed definitions of terms, either in class discussion or on tests. Terminology is just a tool, a useful label for the moment, so that you and the students can talk to each other about English grammar.

Most students benefit from knowing what is going to be covered in the following class session. The students should be assigned to read the charts at home so that they can become familiar with the target structure and, it is to be hoped, come to class with questions.

For every chart, try to relate the target structure to an immediate classroom or "real-life" context. Make up or elicit examples that use the students' names, activities, and interests. The here-and-now classroom context is, of course, one of the grammar teacher's best aids.

Degrees of Teacher and Student Involvement

Most of the exercises in the text are intended to be teacher-led, but other options are group work, pair work, and student-led work.

TEACHER-LED EXERCISES

In an eclectic text such as this, many approaches are possible, based on various sound theories of language learning and teaching. The teacher plays many roles and can employ a wide variety of techniques.

In essence, all exercises in the main text are teacher-led. Even so, there is a wide range of possible teacher involvement: from lecturing on "rules" to eliciting deductive understandings, from supplying answers to eliciting responses, from being the focus of the students' attention to being solely an initiator and facilitator. Consider the students' goals and the time that is available, then decide whether to focus a lot of attention on every item in an exercise or to go through it quickly and spend time on related activities. It is beneficial for students to push hard and work intensively on English grammar, but it is also beneficial for the students to spend relaxed time in class exchanging ideas in structure-oriented conversations or similar pursuits.

GROUP WORK AND PAIR WORK

Many, but not all, exercises in the text are suitable for group or pair work. Suggestions for such alternatives are included in the comments on the exercises in the Chapter Notes in this *Guide*.

Exercises done in groups or pairs may often take twice as much time as they would if teacher-led, but it is time well spent if you plan carefully and make sure that the students are speaking in English to each other. There are many advantages to student–student practice.

When the students are working in groups or pairs, their opportunities to use what they are learning are greatly increased. They will often explain things to each other during pair work, in which case both students benefit. Obviously, the students in group work are often much more active and involved than in teacher-led exercises.

Group and pair work also expands the students' opportunities to practice many communication skills at the same time that they are practicing target structures. In peer interaction in the classroom, the students have to agree, disagree, continue a conversation, make suggestions, promote cooperation, make requests, be sensitive to each other's needs and personalities, and the like—exchanges that are characteristic of any group communication, in the classroom or elsewhere.

In addition, group and pair work helps to produce a comfortable learning environment. In teacher-centered activities, students may sometimes feel shy and inhibited or may experience stress. They may feel that they have to respond quickly and accurately and that *what* they say is not as important as *how* they say it, even though you strive to convince them to the contrary. If you set up groups that are noncompetitive and cooperative, the students usually tend to help, encourage, and even joke with each other. This encourages them to experiment with the language and to speak more.

Students should be encouraged to monitor each other to some extent in group work, especially when monitoring activities are specifically assigned. (But perhaps you should remind them to give some *positive* as well as corrective comments to each other in order to maintain good feelings.) You shouldn't worry about "losing control" of the students' language production, and they shouldn't worry about learning each other's mistakes. Not every mistake needs to be corrected, but you can take some time at the end of an exercise to call attention to mistakes that you heard frequently as you listened in on the groups.

WAYS OF USING EXERCISES FOR GROUP OR PAIR WORK

1. Divide the class into groups of two to six, usually with one student as leader. You may appoint the students to the groups or sometimes let them divide themselves. You may appoint a leader or let the students choose one. Leadership can be rotated. Be sure that the leader understands what to do, and set a reasonable time limit for finishing the activity.

2. For ORAL (BOOKS CLOSED) exercises, only the leader has his/her text open. If these exercises are used for pair work, one student has an open text and the other doesn't. Halfway through an exercise, the pair may change roles.

3. For ORAL or some other types of exercises, the students can discuss completions, transformations, etc., among themselves prior to, or instead of, class discussion. You can move about the classroom answering questions as necessary.

4. For exercises that require writing in the textbook, each group should produce one set of answers that all (or at least a majority) of the members agree are correct. The leader can present the group's answers for class discussion or hand in a collaborative paper for your correction and sometimes even for a grade. Similarly, pairs of students can compare their answers prior to class discussion and come to an agreement on the correctness.

STUDENT-LED EXERCISES

Once in a while you may wish to ask a student to assume the teacher's role in some of the ORAL or ORAL (BOOKS CLOSED) exercises; the student conducts the exercise by giving the cues and determining the appropriateness of the response, while you retire to a corner of the room. It is helpful, but not essential, for you to work with the student leader outside of class in preparation for his/her role as teacher. Usually, a student-led oral exercise will take twice as much class time as a teacher-led exercise, but if the time is available, it can be a valuable experience for the student-teacher and fun for the entire class.

Techniques for Exercise Types

Some of the exercises in the text have specific labels: ORAL (BOOKS CLOSED), ORAL, WRITTEN, ORAL/WRITTEN, ERROR ANALYSIS, PREPOSITIONS, PHRASAL VERBS, PRETEST. It is important to note that the "oral" and "written" labels on particular exercises are only suggestions to the teacher. If you deem it appropriate, you can have the students write out an oral exercise or discuss a written exercise.

Exercise: ORAL (BOOKS CLOSED)

a. For exercises of this type, which range from simple manipulation to open-ended communicative interaction, the students have their books closed. These exercises are not intended as fast-paced drills to be completed without interruption. Their pace should allow ample time for the students to understand and respond as well as enough time for short spontaneous conversations to occur. These exercises provide a good opportunity for the students to develop their listening and speaking skills while expanding their ability to use the target structures. With their books closed, they can concentrate on what you and others are saying and can practice speaking without relying on written words.

b. Be flexible in handling these exercises. You don't have to read the items aloud as though reading a script from which there should be no deviation. Modify the format to make it more workable for your particular class. Try to add more items spontaneously as they occur to you. Change the items in any way to make them more relevant to your students. (For example, if you know that some students plan to watch the World Cup soccer match on TV, include a sentence about that.) Omit irrelevant items. Sometimes an item will start a spontaneous discussion of, for example, local restaurants or current movies or certain experiences the students have had. These spur-of-the-moment dialogues are very beneficial to the students. Encourage and facilitate the discussion, and then, within a reasonable length of time, bring attention back to the grammar at hand.

c. To initiate an ORAL (BOOKS CLOSED) exercise, give the class an example or two of the format. Sometimes you will want to give explicit oral directions. Sometimes you will want to use the chalkboard to write down key words to help the students focus on the target structure or consider the options in their responses.

d. Repeat a cue in ORAL (BOOKS CLOSED) exercises as often as necessary. Start out with normal spoken English, but then slow down and repeat as needed. You may want to write on the board, do a pantomime, demonstrate, draw a picture—whatever may help the students understand what you're saying. One of your goals is to convince students that they *can* understand spoken English. They shouldn't feel failure or be embarrassed if they don't understand a spoken cue immediately. If an exercise is too difficult for your class as a whole or for particular students, let them do it with their books open.

e. In general, ORAL (BOOKS CLOSED) exercises follow a chart or an open-book exercise. First, students should build up their understanding of the structure and practice using it. Then they will feel more confident during these oral exercises, which for many students are riskier and far more difficult than open-book work.

Essentially, in the ORAL (BOOKS CLOSED) exercises, the teacher is saying to the students, "Okay, now you understand such-and-such [for example, word order in noun clauses], so let's play with it a bit. With any luck, you'll be happily surprised by how much you already know. Mistakes are no big problem. They're a natural part of learning a new language. So just give it a try and let's see what happens."

f. Sometimes ORAL (BOOKS CLOSED) exercises precede a chart or open-book exercises. The purpose of this order is to elicit student-generated examples of the target structure as a springboard to the discussion of the grammar. If you prefer to introduce any particular structure to your students orally, you can always use an ORAL (BOOKS CLOSED) exercise prior to the presentation of a chart and written exercises, no matter what the given order is in the textbook.

Exercise: ORAL

Exercises of this type are intended to be done with books open but require no writing and no preparation. In other words, the students can read what is in the text, but they don't have to write in their books. You don't have to assign these exercises ahead of time; they can be done directly in class. These exercises come in many forms and are often suitable for group or pair work.

Exercise: ORAL/WRITTEN

This label indicates that the material can be used for either speaking practice or writing practice. Sometimes it indicates that the two are combined: e.g., a speaking activity may lead to a writing activity.

Exercise: WRITTEN

In this type of exercise, the students should use their own paper and submit their answers to you. Some of the WRITTEN exercises require sentence completion, but most are designed to produce short, informal compositions. In general, the topics or tasks concern aspects of the students' lives in order to encourage free and relatively effortless communication as they practice their writing skills. While a course in English rhetoric is beyond the scope of this text, many of the basic elements are included and may be developed and emphasized according to your purposes.

For best results, whenever you make a writing assignment, let your students know what you expect: "This is what I suggest as content. This is how you might organize it. This is how long I expect it to be." It is always a good idea for you to sit down and write an assignment yourself before discussing it with the class. If at all possible, give your students composition models, perhaps taken from good compositions written by previous classes, perhaps written by you, perhaps composed as a group activity by the class as a whole (e.g., you write on the board what the students tell you to write, and then you and the students revise it together).

In general, WRITTEN exercises should be done outside of class. All of us need time to consider and revise when we write. The topics in the exercises are structured so that plagiarism should not be a problem. Use in-class writing if you want to appraise the students' unaided, spontaneous writing skills. Tell your students that these written exercises are simply for practice and that— even though they should always try to do their best—mistakes that occur will be considered only as opportunities for learning.

Encourage the students to use their dictionaries whenever they write. Point out that you yourself never write seriously without a dictionary at hand. Discuss the use of margins, indentation of paragraphs, and other aspects of the format of a well-written paper.

Ask your students to use lined paper and to write on every other line, so that you and they have space to make corrections. APPENDIX 3 presents a system for marking errors so that students may make their own corrections and so that you may mark papers quickly and efficiently. (See p. xviii of this *Guide* for information about using APPENDIX 3.)

Exercise: ERROR ANALYSIS

For the most part, the sentences in this type of exercise have been adapted from actual student writing and contain typical errors. ERROR ANALYSIS exercises focus on the target structures of a chapter but may also contain miscellaneous errors that are common in student writing at this level, such as omission of final -*s* on plural nouns or capitalization of proper nouns. The purpose of including them is to sharpen the students' self-monitoring skills.

ERROR ANALYSIS exercises are challenging and fun, a good way to summarize the grammar in a chapter. If you wish, tell the students they are either newspaper editors or English teachers; their task is to locate all mistakes and write corrections.

The recommended technique is to assign an ERROR ANALYSIS for in-class discussion the next day. The students benefit most from having the opportunity to find the errors themselves prior to class discussion. These exercises can, of course, be handled in other ways: seatwork, written homework, group work, pair work.

Some teachers object to allowing students to see errors written in a textbook. However, there is little chance that any harm is being done. Students look at errors all the time in their own writing and profit from finding and correcting them. The benefits of doing ERROR ANALYSIS exercises far outweigh any possible (and highly unlikely) negative results. Point out that even native speakers or highly proficient non-native speakers—including you yourself—have to scrutinize, correct, and revise what they write. This is a natural part of the writing process.

Exercise: PREPOSITIONS

Exercises of this type focus on prepositions that combine with verbs and adjectives. The intention is that the students simply make their "best guess" according to what "sounds right" to them when completing each item, then get the correct answers from class discussion and learn the ones they missed. They can refer to the list of combinations in APPENDIX 2 if they want to.

To reinforce the prepositions in an exercise, you can make up quick oral reviews (books closed) by rephrasing the items and having the students call out the prepositions. For example:

Text entry: I subscribe __*to*__ several magazines.
Made-up oral reinforcement exercise:
    TEACHER: "I like to read magazines. I subscribe . . . ."
    STUDENTS call out: "to"
    TEACHER: "Good. Subscribe **to**. I subscribe **to** several magazines."

Text entry: Do you believe __*in*__ ghosts?
Made-up oral reinforcement exercise:
    TEACHER: "I'm not convinced that ghosts exist. What about you? Do you believe . . . ."
    STUDENTS call out: "in"
    TEACHER: "Right. Believe **in**. Do you believe **in** ghosts?"

Exercise: PHRASAL VERBS

These contain two- and three-word verbs and can be handled in the same ways as the PREPOSITIONS exercises, adding increased emphasis on discussion of the phrases as vocabulary items.

As with the PREPOSITIONS exercises, the PHRASAL VERBS exercises are interspersed throughout the text at the ends of chapters. The intention is that the students review and/or learn a few of the most common of these expressions at a time. The scope and length of the text do not allow for an intensive treatment of the hundreds of phrasal verbs in the English language.

The term "adverb particle" is not used in the text, as it is deemed a possible source of confusion and unnecessary for the students' purposes.

Exercise: PRETEST

The purpose of these exercises is to let the students discover what they do and do not know about the target structure in order to get them interested in a chart. Essentially, PRETEST exercises illustrate a possible teaching technique: quiz the students first as a springboard for presenting the grammar in a chart.

Additional Techniques

Most of the exercises in the textbook do not have specific labels. The following section outlines additional techniques not only for labeled exercises but also for other activities.

The majority of the exercises in the text require some sort of completion, transformation, combination, discussion of meaning, or a combination of such activities. They range from those that are tightly controlled and manipulative to those that encourage free responses and require creative, independent language use. The techniques vary according to the exercise type.

FILL-IN-THE-BLANKS AND CONTROLLED COMPLETION EXERCISES

The label "fill-in-the-blanks" refers to those exercises in which the students complete the sentences by using words given in parentheses. The label "controlled completion" refers to those exercises in which the students complete sentences using the words in a given list. Both types of exercises call for similar techniques.

Technique A: A student can be asked to read an item aloud. You can say whether the student's answer is correct or not, or you can open up discussion by asking the rest of the class if the answer is correct. For example:

TEACHER: "Juan, would you please read Number 2?"
STUDENT: "Diane *washes* her hair every other day or so."
TEACHER (to the class): "Do the rest of you agree with Juan's answer?"

The slow-moving pace of this method is beneficial for discussion not only of grammar items but also of vocabulary and content. The students have time to digest information and ask questions. You have the opportunity to judge how well they understand the grammar.

However, this time-consuming technique doesn't always, or even usually, need to be used, especially with more advanced classes.

Technique B: You, the teacher, read the first part of the item, then pause for the students to call out the answer in unison. For example:

Text entry: Diane (*wash*) _____ her hair every other day or so.
TEACHER (with the students looking at their texts): "Diane . . . ."
STUDENTS (in unison): "washes" (plus possibly a few incorrect responses scattered about)
TEACHER: ". . . washes her hair every other day or so. *Washes.* Do you have any questions?"

This technique saves a lot of time in class and is slow-paced enough to allow for questions and discussion of grammar, vocabulary, and content. It is essential that the students have prepared the exercise by writing in their books, so it must be assigned ahead as homework.

Technique C: With an advanced class for whom a particular exercise is little more than a quick review, you can simply give the answers so the students can correct their own previously prepared work in their textbooks. You can either read the whole sentence ("Number 2: Diane washes her hair every other day or so") or just give the answer ("Number 2: washes"). You can give the answers to the items one at a time, taking questions as they arise, or give the answers to the whole exercise before opening it up for questions. As an alternative, you can have one of the students read his/her answers and have the other students ask him/her questions if they disagree.

Technique D: Divide the class into groups (or pairs) and have each group prepare one set of answers that they all agree is correct prior to class discussion. The leader of each group can present their answers.

Another option is to have the groups (or pairs) hand in their set of answers for correction and possibly a grade.

It's also possible to turn these exercises into games wherein the group with the best set of answers gets some sort of reward (perhaps applause from the rest of the class).

Of course, you can always mix Techniques A, B, C, and D—with the students reading some aloud, with you prompting unison response for some, with you simply giving the answers for others, with the students collaborating on the answers for others. Much depends on the level of the class, their familiarity and skill with the grammar at hand, their oral-aural skills in general, and how flexible or limited your available classtime is.

Technique E: When an exercise item has a dialogue between speakers A and B, ask one student to be A and another B and have them read the entry aloud. Then, occasionally, say to A and B: "Without looking at your text, what did you just say to each other?" (If necessary, let them glance briefly at their texts before they repeat what they've just said in the exercise item.) The students may be pleasantly surprised by their own fluency.

OPEN COMPLETION EXERCISES

The term "open completion" refers to those exercises in which the students use their own words to complete the sentences.

Technique A: Exercises where the students must supply their own words to complete a sentence should usually be assigned for out-of-class preparation. Then in class, one, two, or several students can read their sentences aloud; the class can discuss the correctness and appropriateness of the completions. Perhaps you can suggest possible ways of rephrasing to make a sentence more idiomatic. Students who don't read their sentences aloud can revise their own completions based on what is being discussed in class. At the end of the exercise discussion, you can tell the students to hand in their sentences for you to look at, or merely ask if anyone has questions about the exercise and not have the students submit anything to you.

Technique B: If you wish to use an open completion exercise in class without having previously assigned it, you can turn the exercise into a brainstorming session in which students try out several completions to see if they work. As another possibility, you may divide the students into small groups and have each group come up with completions that they all agree are correct and appropriate. Then use only these completions for class discussion or as written work to be handed in.

Technique C: Some open completion exercises are designated WRITTEN, which usually means the students need to use their own paper, as not enough space has been left in the textbook. It is often beneficial to use the following progression: (1) assign the exercise for out-of-class preparation; (2) discuss it in class the next day, having the students make corrections on their own papers based on what they are learning from discussing other students' completions; (3) then ask the students to submit their papers to you, either as a requirement or on a volunteer basis.

TRANSFORMATION AND COMBINATION EXERCISES

In transformation exercises, the students are asked to change form but not substance (e.g., to change the active to the passive, a clause to a phrase, or a question to a noun clause).

In combination exercises, the students are asked to combine two or more sentences or ideas into one sentence that contains a particular structure (e.g., an adjective clause, a parallel structure, a gerund phrase).

In general, these exercises, which require manipulation of a form, are intended for class discussion of the form and meaning of a structure. The initial stages of such exercises are a good opportunity to use the chalkboard to draw circles and arrows to illustrate the characteristics and relationships of a structure. Students can read their answers aloud to initiate the class discussion, and you can write on the board as problems arise. Another possibility is to have the students write their sentences on the board. Also possible is to have them work in small groups to agree upon their answers prior to class discussion.

DISCUSSION-OF-MEANING EXERCISES

Some exercises consist primarily of you and the students discussing the meaning of given sentences. Most of these exercises ask the students to compare the meaning of two or more sentences (for example, *You should take an English course* vs. *You must take an English course*). One of the main purposes of discussion-of-meaning exercises is to provide an opportunity for summary comparison of the structures in a particular unit.

The basic technique in these exercises is for you to pose questions about the given sentences and then let the students explain what a structure means to them (which allows you to get input about what they do and do not understand). Then you summarize the salient points as necessary. Students have their own inventive, creative way of explaining differences in meaning. They shouldn't be expected to sound like grammar teachers. Often, all you need to do is listen carefully and patiently to a student's explanation, and then clarify and reinforce it by rephrasing it somewhat.

PRONUNCIATION EXERCISES

A few exercises focus on pronunciation of grammatical features, such as endings on nouns or verbs and contracted or reduced forms.

Some phonetic symbols are used in these exercises to point out sounds that should not be pronounced identically; for example, /s/, /əz/, and /z/ represent the three predictable pronunciations of the grammatical suffix spelled -*s* or -*es*. It is not necessary for students to learn a complete phonetic alphabet; they should merely associate each symbol in an exercise with a sound that is different from all others. The purpose is to help students become more aware of these final sounds in the English they hear to encourage proficiency of use in their own speaking and writing.

In the exercises on spoken contractions, the primary emphasis should be on the students' hearing and becoming familiar with spoken forms rather than on their production of these forms. The students need to understand that what they see in writing is not exactly what they should expect to hear in normal, rapid spoken English. The most important point of most of these exercises is that the students listen to your oral production and become familiar with the reduced forms.

Language learners are naturally conscious that their pronunciation is not like that of native speakers of the language. Therefore, some of them are embarrassed or shy about speaking. In a pronunciation exercise, they may be more comfortable if you ask groups or the whole class to say a sentence in unison. After that, individuals may volunteer to speak the same sentence. The learners' production does not need to be perfect, just understandable. You can encourage the students to be less inhibited by having them teach you how to pronounce words in their languages (unless, of course, you're a native speaker of the students' language in a monolingual class). It's fun—and instructive—for the students to teach the teacher.

SEATWORK

It is generally preferable to assign exercises for out-of-class preparation, but sometimes it's necessary to cover an exercise in class that you haven't been able to assign previously. In "seatwork," you have the students do an unassigned exercise in class immediately before discussing it. Seatwork allows the students to try an exercise themselves before the answers are discussed so that they can discover what problems they may be having with a particular structure. Seatwork may be done individually, in pairs, or in groups.

HOMEWORK

The textbook assumes that the students will have the opportunity to prepare most of the exercises by writing in their books prior to class discussion. Students should be assigned this homework as a matter of course.

The use of the term "written homework" in this *Guide* suggests that the students write out an exercise on their own paper and hand it in to you. How much written homework you have the students do is up to you. The amount generally depends upon such variables as class size, class level, available classtime, your available paper-correcting time, not to mention your preferences in teaching techniques.

Most of the exercises in the text can be handled through class discussion without the necessity of the students' handing in written homework. By combining the *Workbook* with the main text, students can regularly do homework that they can correct themselves. Most of the written homework to be handed in that is suggested in the text and in the chapter notes in this *Guide* consists of activities that will produce original, independent writing.

CORRECTING WRITING ERRORS

APPENDIX 3 in *Understanding and Using English Grammar* (pp. A29–A30 in the back of the text) presents a system for marking errors in students' written work. It uses a numbering scheme for the purpose of signaling errors. This system is quite flexible, intended only to give the students hints when they set about correcting their own writing.

Some of the numbers have multiple uses. For example, 2 (Wrong Form) can signal that an adjective has been used instead of an adverb, a noun instead of an adjective, a gerund instead of an infinitive, incorrect *has being done* instead of *has been done*, incorrect *would has* instead of *would have*, etc. Other numbers have more limited uses. For example, 13 is intended only for run-on sentences or comma splices.

Some errors could be marked by either of two numbers. For example, *to*, as in *The weather is to cold*, could be marked by either 3 (Wrong Word) or 8 (Spelling). The word *beautifuls*, as in *I saw some beautifuls pictures*, could be marked by either 1 (Singular-Plural) or 2 (Wrong Form). Simply choose the number that you think will give the student the best help in correcting and learning from the mistake in that context.

For some errors, it is necessary to use two numbers in the same circle. For example, the word *intresting*, as in *I am intresting in that subject*, could be marked by both 8 (Spelling) and 2 (Wrong Form).

Write the full correction for any error that you are sure the student would be unable to correct himself/herself. When necessary, write a more idiomatic phrase. Use 12? (Meaning Not Clear) when you want the student to find a different way to express what s/he is trying to say, or when the handwriting is illegible.

Using the numbers soon becomes automatic, and marking papers proceeds quickly and efficiently.

Reviewing the corrections made later by the students also proceeds smoothly, especially if they have written the original composition on every other line, have left adequate margins, and have used a pen or pencil of a different color to make the corrections. Compositions with numerous errors should be rewritten entirely.

You may wish to add numbers to the list to specify particular problems with structure or style. For example, 14 could suggest Parallel Structure; 15 could denote Repetitiveness. The numbers given in APPENDIX 3 have been distilled from many to a few through years of experimentation, but the system is still adaptable.

Using the *Workbook*

The *Workbook* contains two kinds of exercises: Selfstudy and Guided Study. The answer key for the Selfstudy Practices is found at the end of the *Workbook* on perforated pages. Encourage your students to remove this answer key and put it in some sort of folder. It's much easier for the students to correct their own answers if they make their own answer key booklet. The answers to the Guided Study Practices are in this *Guide*.

The *Workbook* mirrors the main text. Exercises are called "exercises" in the main text and "practices" in the workbook to minimize confusion when you make assignments. Each practice in the *Workbook* has a content title and refers the students to appropriate charts in the main text.

In the chapter notes in this *Guide*, you will find the notation "◇ **WORKBOOK**" followed by the practices that can be assigned at or near that point in the lesson.

SELFSTUDY PRACTICES (ANSWERS GIVEN IN THE *WORKBOOK*)

Answers to the Selfstudy Practices are included in the *Workbook* so that students can immediately check their understanding and accuracy. The primary purpose of the Selfstudy Practices is to give the students ample opportunity to understand and use the target structures on their own. They should be encouraged to bring any questions about the Selfstudy Practices to class.

Selfstudy Practices can be assigned by you or, depending upon the level of maturity or sense of purpose of the class, simply left for the students to use as they wish. They may be assigned to the entire class or only to those students who need further practice with a particular structure. They may be used as reinforcement after you have covered a chart and exercises in class or as introductory material prior to discussing a chart in class.

In addition, the students can use the Selfstudy Practices to acquaint themselves with the grammar of any units not covered in class. Earnest students can use the *Workbook* to teach themselves.

GUIDED STUDY PRACTICES (ANSWERS NOT GIVEN IN THE *WORKBOOK*)

Answers to the Guided Study practices are given only in this *Teacher's Guide* for two reasons: (1) because many of the answers depend on students' creativity and require the teacher's judgment, and (2) so that some of the practices can be used as supplementary teaching materials for class use, written homework, individualized instruction, or possibly as quizzes.

PRACTICE TESTS IN THE *WORKBOOK*

Each chapter in the *Workbook* has Practice Test A (Selfstudy) and Practice Test B (Guided Study). You may wish to use one as a "pretest" and the other as a "post-test," or simply use both of them as summary review material upon finishing a chapter.

The practice tests are not really intended as "tests." They are simply another exercise type, to be used as a teaching tool like any other exercise. The students should simply be encouraged to do their best and learn from their mistakes.

You may, however, wish to have the students take a practice test in class under time-pressure conditions for experience in taking that kind of test. (Allow 30 seconds per item.) You could also have the students time themselves if they do the practice test at home.

Notes on American vs. British English

Students are often curious about differences between American and British English. They should know that the differences are minor. Anyone who has studied British English (BrE) should have no trouble adapting to American English (AmE), and vice versa.

DIFFERENCES IN GRAMMAR

Many of the differences in grammar are either footnoted in the main text or mentioned in the chart notes in this *Guide*. For example, the footnote to Chart 5-18 contains the information that BrE uses a plural verb with *government* whereas AmE uses a singular verb. Similarly, the notes in this *Guide* for Chart 2-11 contain the information that *don't let's* is considered incorrect in AmE but is acceptable informal usage in BrE. Teachers need to be careful not to inadvertently mark usage differences as errors; rather, they should simply point out to the students that a difference exists between two equally correct varieties of English.

Differences in article and preposition usage in certain common expressions follow. These differences are not noted in the text; they are given here for the teacher's information. The symbol Ø denotes that "nothing" is used there.

AmE	BrE
*be in **the** hospital*	*be in Ø hospital*
*be at **the** university (be in Ø college)*	*be at Ø university*
*go to **a** university (go to Ø college)*	*go to Ø university*
go to Ø class/be in Ø class	*go to **a** class/be in **a** class*
*in **the** future*	*in Ø future (OR in **the** future)*
*did it **the** next day*	*did it Ø next day (OR **the** next day)*
*haven't done something **for/in** weeks*	*haven't done something **for** weeks*
*ten minutes **past/after** six o'clock*	*ten minutes **past** six o'clock*
*five minutes **to/of/til** seven o'clock*	*five minutes **to** seven o'clock*

DIFFERENCES IN SPELLING

Variant spellings can be noted but should not be marked as incorrect in the students' writing. Spelling differences in some common words follow.

AmE	BrE
jewelry, traveler, woolen	*jewellry, traveller, woollen*
skillful, fulfill, installment	*skilful, fulfil, instalment*
color, honor, labor, odor	*colour, honour, labour, odour*
realize, analyze, apologize	*realise, analyse, apologise*
defense, offense, license	*defence, offence, licence (n.)*
theater, center, liter	*theatre, centre, litre*
check	*cheque (bank note)*
curb	*kerb*
forever	*for ever/forever*
jail	*gaol*
program	*programme*
specialty	*speciality*
story	*storey (of a building)*
tire	*tyre*
spilled, dreamed, burned	*spilt, dreamt, burnt (See the footnote to Chart 1-11.)*

DIFFERENCES IN VOCABULARY

Differences in vocabulary usage usually do not significantly interfere with communication. Students should know that when American and British speakers read each other's literature, they encounter only very few differences in vocabulary usage. A few differences between AmE and BrE follow.

AmE	BrE	AmE	BrE
attorney, lawyer	*barrister, solicitor*	*fired/laid off*	*made redundant*
bathrobe	*dressing gown*	*living room*	*sitting room, drawing room*
can (of beans)	*tin (of beans)*	*raise in salary*	*rise in salary*
cookie, cracker	*biscuit*	*rest room*	*public toilet, WC (water closet)*
corn	*maize*	*schedule*	*timetable*
diaper	*nappy*	*sidewalk*	*pavement, footpath*
driver's license	*driving licence*	*sink*	*basin*
drug store	*chemist's*	*soccer*	*football*
elevator	*lift*	*stove*	*cooker*
eraser	*rubber*	*truck*	*lorry, van*
flashlight	*torch*	*trunk of a car*	*boot of a motorcar*
gas, gasoline	*petrol*	*be on vacation*	*be on holiday*
hood of a car	*bonnet of a motorcar*		

Key to Pronunciation Symbols

THE PHONETIC ALPHABET (Symbols for American English)

CONSONANTS

Most consonant symbols are used phonetically as they are in normal English spelling. However, a few additional symbols are needed, and some other letters are more restricted in their use as symbols. These special symbols are presented below. (Note that slanted lines indicate that phonetic symbols, not the spelling alphabet, are being used.)

/Θ/ (Greek theta) = voiceless *th* as in "**th**in," "**th**ank"
/δ/ (Greek delta) = voiced *th* as in "**th**en," "**th**ose"
/ŋ/ = *ng* as in "si**ng**," "thi**ng**" (but not in "danger")
/š/ = *sh* as in "**sh**irt," "mi**ss**ion," "na**t**ion"
/ž/ = *s* or *z* in a few words like "plea**s**ure," "a**z**ure"
/č/ = *ch* or *tch* as in "wa**tch**," "**ch**urch"
/ǰ/ = *j* or *dge* as in "**j**ump," "le**dge**"

The following consonants are used as in *conventional spelling:*

/b, d, f, g, h, k, l, m, n, p, r, s, t, v, w, y, z/

Spelling consonants that are **not** used phonetically in English: c, q, x

VOWELS

The 5 vowels in the spelling alphabet are inadequate to represent the 12–15 vowel sounds of American speech. Therefore, new symbols and new sound associations for familiar letters must be adopted.

Front	**Central**	**Back** (lips rounded)
/i/ or /iy/ as in "**bea**t"		/u/, /u:/, or /uw/ as in "**boo**t"
/ɪ/ as in "**bi**t"		/ʊ/ as in "**boo**k"
/e/ or /ey/ as in "**bai**t"		/o/ or /ow/ as in "**boa**t"
		/ɔ/ as in "**bough**t"
/ɛ/ as in "**be**t"	/ə/ as in "**bu**t"	
/æ/ as in "**ba**t"	/a/ as in "**bo**ther"	

GLIDES: /ai/ or /ay/ as in "**bi**te"
/ɔi/ or /ɔy/ as in "**bo**y"
/au/ or /aw/ as in "ab**ou**t"

British English has a somewhat different set of vowel sounds and symbols. You might want to consult a standard pronunciation text for that system.

UNDERSTANDING AND USING

ENGLISH GRAMMAR
Second Edition

TEACHER'S GUIDE
Volume A

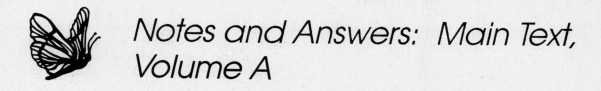

Notes and Answers: Main Text, Volume A

Chapter 1: VERB TENSES

ORDER OF CHAPTER	CHARTS	EXERCISES	WORKBOOK
First day of class talking/writing		Ex. 1 → 2	
Overview of verb tenses	1-1 → 1-5	Ex. 3 → 4	Pr. 1 → 3
Spelling of -ing and -ed forms	1-6	Ex. 5 → 9	Pr. 4
Simple present/present progressive	1-7 → 1-10	Ex. 10 → 14	Pr. 5 → 7
Simple past/past progressive	1-11 → 1-14	Ex. 15 → 23	Pr. 8 → 17
Cumulative review and practice		Ex. 24 → 25	
Present perfect/ present perfect progressive	1-15 → 1-16	Ex. 26 → 37	Pr. 18 → 24
Past perfect/past perfect progressive	1-17 → 1-18	Ex. 38 → 41	Pr. 25 → 29
Cumulative review and practice		Ex. 42 → 44	
Future time	1-19 → 1-25	Ex. 45 → 51	Pr. 30 → 38
Cumulative review and practice		Ex. 52 → 65	Pr. 39 → 44 Pr. Tests A & B

General Notes on Chapter 1

• OBJECTIVE: This chapter begins with an overview of all twelve of the English verb tenses. The intention is for the students to understand that somewhat logical relationships do exist among the tenses, i.e., that there is some predictability to the tense system in English.

• APPROACH: Students using this text are probably somewhat familiar with all the verb tenses (with the possible exception of the future perfect and future perfect progressive, two little-used tenses). In presenting the initial charts in this chapter, you can help the learners understand the overall patterns in the English tense system (that all progressive tenses indicate that an activity is/was/will be in progress, for example, or that all perfect tenses indicate that one activity occurs before another activity or time). Then as you concentrate on each tense in turn as you proceed through the chapter, you can refer to Chart 1-5 to put each tense within the framework of English verb tenses. For example, you can relate the use of the past progressive *(I was sitting in class at this time yesterday)* to the present progressive *(I am sitting in class right now)*.

• TERMINOLOGY: The text calls all twelve of the verb forms in Chart 1-5 "tenses." Some other analyses of the English verb system may propose that there are only two tenses: past and non-past. They may use the term "aspect" for the perfective and progressive forms.

In this text, the term "tense" is deemed useful to both you and the students because it is a relatively easy and traditional term to use pedagogically to identify twelve verb forms that have particular meanings and uses within a relational system. Whatever these twelve forms are called, the only important consideration for the student is their meaning and use. In sum, it is helpful for purposes of teacher-student communication for the students to learn the "names" of the "tenses," but one should never lose sight of the fact that almost all grammar labels are simply a means to an end, not an end in themselves, in the ESL/EFL classroom.

☐ **EXERCISE 1, p. 1.** *Getting to know each other the first day of class.*

TECHNIQUE: *Oral, teacher-led; followed by pair work.*★

First, ask students to suggest questions for topics in the list. Try to elicit idiomatic questions—forms that a native speaker of English would normally use in this situation.

Next, divide the class into pairs, if possible mixing language groups in a multilingual class or mixing proficiency levels in a monolingual class. Discuss two ways to conduct the interview: (1) Student A completes the entire interview of Student B, then Student B conducts an interview of Student A; or (2) Students A and B take turns asking about each topic.

Give the class 10 to 15 minutes for the interviews. Then ask each student to introduce his/her interviewee, giving the person's name and interesting comments about him or her. Either the student or you should write the interviewee's name on the chalkboard. The rest of the class should be encouraged to write down the names of their classmates as a way to start getting to know each other.

As followup to the in-class activity, you could ask the students to write the information from their interviews in a short composition (in class or out of class) and hand it in.

EXPANSION ACTIVITY: Assign pairs or small groups of students to go someplace together before or during the next class period and write a report of their experiences. (They could go to an eating place near the school, to a park, to a particular landmark in the city. Remind them to use only English.) You may also wish to have the students use their experiences for oral reports. If you assign the students different places to go, the subsequent oral reports can serve to provide the class as a whole with information about their surroundings.

ASSUMPTIONS: This exercise assumes that students know how to ask and answer basic questions in English. (You may wish to give a "short course" in question word order if the need arises during class discussion, but primarily this first exercise in class is not intended to focus on any particular grammar. You may, however, wish to refer the students to Appendix 1, Unit B (Questions) if problems such as word order arise, or use that unit as a followup to this exercise.) This exercise also assumes that the students don't know each other. If all the students are already acquainted, they could pretend to be famous persons being interviewed by television or newspaper reporters and make up entirely different questions.

★ See the INTRODUCTION: *Classroom Techniques* (pp. ix–xviii) for descriptions of possible techniques to use in the various kinds of exercises: *written, oral (books closed), fill-in-the-blanks, completion,* etc., and ways of handling teacher and student involvement: *teacher-led, student-led, group work, pair work.*

POSSIBLE ANSWERS:
1. What is your name? [Compare with "What do you call yourself?" or "How are you called?", grammatically correct but idiomatically inappropriate questions.]
2. How do you spell your (last) name?/How do you spell that? [Discuss cultural naming systems: What is a first name, middle name, last name, given name, surname, maiden name?]
3. Where are you from? / What country are you from? / What is your hometown? / Where were you born?
4. Where are you living? / Where do you live?
5. How long have you been living in (*name of this city or town*)/living here? How long do you plan to be/are you planning to be/are you going to be in (*name of this city or town*)/be here?
6. Why did you (decide to) come here?
7. [If a student]: What is your major/your field of study? / What are you studying?
   [If an employee]: What kind of work do you do? / What do you do for a living?
8. What do you like to do in your spare time? / Do you have any hobbies?
9. How are you getting along?
10. How do you like living here?/What do you think of (*name of this city or town*)?

☐ **EXERCISE 2, p. 1.** *Using present, past, and future tenses in writing.*

TECHNIQUE: *Written.*★

Discuss what you want the composition to contain before the students begin writing—for example: basic biographical information (name, place of origin, family, education and/or work, etc.); places of residence, travel, and other activities in the past two years; plans for the immediate future (school, work, places of residence, etc.).

ALTERNATIVE: Instead of an autobiography, each student could write a biography of the person s/he interviewed or another person in the class. This would require an additional interview session concerning present, past, and future activities.

◇ **WORKBOOK:** You may wish to have the students do Practice Test A (Chapter 1) at this point, or save Test A for summary review at the end of the chapter.

☐ **EXERCISE 3, p. 1.** *Oral survey of verb tenses.*

TECHNIQUE: *Oral (books closed), teacher-led.*★

This is not a drill or a test. It is a launching pad, so to speak. If you wish, you can use this exercise to introduce almost all the essential information contained in Charts 1-1 through 1-5 by discussing each item in detail and presenting the diagram of tenses that appears in the following charts. Or you can simply use this exercise as a quick run-through of the tenses prior to your presentation of Charts 1-1 through 1-5.

Do the exercise with books open if your class seems to be having a lot of difficulty understanding and remembering what you are saying when you give them the cues. Otherwise, begin now to get your students used to handling oral interaction without depending upon reading what is written in the text.

EXPECTED QUESTIONS: **1.** A: What do you do every day before you come to school?
2. A: What did you do last night? **3.** A: What have you done/have you been doing since you got up this morning? [Even though the present perfect progressive is possible, try to elicit the present perfect in item 5 so that you can compare its use with that of the present perfect progressive in item 6.] **4.** A: What are you doing right now (at exactly 9:17 A.M.)?
5. A: What were you doing at exactly (9:17 A.M.) yesterday? **6.** A: What have you been doing for the past five minutes? **7.** A: What will you do/are you going to do tomorrow?
8. A: What will you be doing/are you going to be doing at exactly (9:23 A.M.) tomorrow?
9. A: What had you done by the time you got to class today? **10.** A: What will you have done

---

★ Throughout this *Teacher's Guide*, see the INTRODUCTION for descriptions of suggested techniques, pp. ix–xviii.

by the time you go to bed tonight?   [Suggestion: Continue the exercise by repeating the cues in random order, perhaps changing the wording slightly. Also, the past perfect progressive and the future perfect progressive are not included in this exercise. You may add them if you wish.]

CHARTS 1-1 through 1-5: OVERVIEW OF VERB TENSES

• The purpose of these charts is to help the students understand the relationships in form and meaning among verb tenses. Discuss the examples, explain the diagrams, summarize tense forms and meanings, and ask for additional examples from the class.

• Not all possible uses of each tense are included in these charts. Tense information is expanded in the individual charts for each tense later in the chapter.

• In Chart 1-5, point out the tense relationships both vertically and horizontally, especially for the progressive, perfect, and perfect progressive forms and meanings.

• Perhaps make a wall chart or transparency of Chart 1-5 for reference during class discussions throughout the time spent on Chapter 1.

• See the INTRODUCTION to this *Guide* (pp. ix–x) for suggestions for presenting the grammar charts.

☐ **EXERCISE 4, p. 8.**   *Oral survey of verb tenses.*

TECHNIQUE: *Oral (books closed), teacher-led.*
     As problems occur, lead a discussion of verb tenses that summarizes the information in the preceding charts. Call attention to time expressions such as *right now, since, before, by the time.* Show how the meanings of these expressions are related to the meanings of the verb tenses.
     ALTERNATIVE: *Pair work or group work.*

◇ **WORKBOOK:** Practices 1, 2, 3.

☐ **EXERCISE 5, p. 8.**   *Spelling of -ing and -ed forms.*

TECHNIQUE: *Pretest.*
     Follow the example: say the word, then a complete sentence, then the word again. Students write only the word on their papers.
     At the end, they can correct their own or each other's papers as you or the students write on the chalkboard. Discuss spelling rules as the papers are being corrected. The order of this exercise mirrors the order of the spelling rules presented in Chart 1-6.
     ALTERNATIVE: You may wish to tell the students to correct their own papers by referring to Chart 1-6 before you discuss the answers with the class.

POSSIBLE SENTENCES: [Use sentences about yourself and your students whenever possible. These sentences are here just in case you need them.]   **1.** Hoped. Maria **hoped** to finish her work early last night. Hoped.   **2.** Dining. I was **dining** with Ali when Kim called. Dining. **3.** Stopped. My clock **stopped** at noon yesterday. Stopped.   **4.** Planning. Olga has been **planning** her vacation for weeks. Planning. [and so on]   **5.** It **rained** last Thursday. **6.** We've been **waiting** for a letter for weeks.   **7.** I've been **listening** to your pronunciation this week.   **8.** What **happened** after class yesterday?   **9.** Your spelling is **beginning** to improve.   **10.** Do you remember what **occurred** on July 8th?   **11.** Pierre is **starting** to enjoy living here.   **12.** The teacher **warned** the students not to be late for class.   **13.** Everyone **enjoyed** Somchart's party last weekend.   **14.** Hiroshi was **playing** loud music at midnight. **15.** How long have you been **studying** English?   **16.** Ms. Lee **worried** about her exams. **17.** My great-grandfather **died** many years ago.   **18.** Carlos was **lying** on the floor when I walked into the room.

CHART 1-6: SPELLING OF *-ING* AND *-ED* FORMS

• Briefly discuss the spelling rule illustrated by each group of examples so that the students become familiar with the content of the chart and can use it for later reference as needed.

• Discuss this chart in conjunction with giving the correct answers to Exercise 5.

☐ **EXERCISES 6 → 9, p. 10.** *Spelling practice of -ing and -ed forms.*

TECHNIQUE: *Seatwork.*

Complete one exercise at a time. Give students a few minutes to write the answers, then have them check their own work or each other's. Either students or the teacher can supply answers, preferably written on the chalkboard.

Even if the students don't know the meaning of some of the words in these exercises, they should be able to spell the forms correctly. After the students have written the correct forms, supply vocabulary definitions for the class as necessary.

ALTERNATIVES: *Pair or group work. Written homework.*

EX. 6 ANSWERS: **2.** hiding **3.** running **4.** ruining **5.** coming **6.** writing **7.** eating **8.** sitting **9.** acting **10.** patting **11.** opening **12.** beginning **13.** earning **14.** frying **15.** dying **16.** employing

EX. 7 ANSWERS: **2.** trying, tried **3.** staying, stayed **4.** taping, taped **5.** tapping, tapped **6.** offering, offered **7.** preferring, preferred **8.** gaining, gained **9.** planning, planned **10.** tying, tied **11.** helping, helped **12.** studying, studied **13.** admitting, admitted **14.** visiting, visited **15.** hugging, hugged **16.** raging, raged

EX. 8 ANSWERS: **1.** bored **2.** jarred **3.** jeered **4.** intensified **5.** sobbed **6.** looted **7.** pointed **8.** ripened **9.** referred **10.** destroyed

EX. 9 ANSWERS: **1.** raiding **2.** riding **3.** bidding **4.** burying **5.** lying **6.** arguing **7.** taming **8.** teeming **9.** trimming **10.** harming

◇ **WORKBOOK:** Practice 4.

CHARTS 1-7 and 1-8: SIMPLE PRESENT AND PRESENT PROGRESSIVE

• Now that the students have covered preliminary material on the English tense system and spelling of *-ing* and *-ed* forms, the text focuses on each tense in more detail.

• Throughout the rest of Chapter 1, the exercises contain questions, negatives, contractions, and midsentence adverbs. These topics are assumed to be primarily review at this level, but the students still need work with them. You may wish to refer your students to Appendix 1 for more information about these topics, or fit the Appendix 1 units into your class instruction as you see the need and find the time.

EXERCISE 10, p. 12. *Simple present vs. present progressive.*

TECHNIQUE: *Fill-in-the-blanks.**

ANSWERS: **1.** is washing   **2.** washes   **3.** usually sits . . . is sitting   **4.** am trying
5. Do you always lock   **6.** am still waiting   **7.** is shining   **8.** shines . . . wakes
9. is snowing . . . doesn't snow   **10.** isn't going . . . attends . . . usually has . . . is working

EXERCISE 11, p. 12. *Using present progressive.*

TECHNIQUE: *Oral.*

Students write one action on a piece of paper. You collect those papers and redistribute them around the class. If the class is very large, this can be done in small groups. A student, without saying anything, performs the action on his/her piece of paper, and another person describes the activity using the present progressive. This is a lively technique for involving several language skills while using English to describe something that is actually happening.

CHART 1-9: NONPROGRESSIVE VERBS

• The key point is the difference between "states" and "activities." No verb is inherently "nonprogressive." The intention of this chart and its terminology is simply to inform the students that certain common verbs are usually not used in the progressive.

• In the list of nonprogressive verbs, even the verbs without asterisks can, usually only in fairly rare circumstances, be used in the progressive. The text, however, concentrates only on the usual, most frequent use of these words. (For example: "I am loving being on vacation" is possible. The more usual usage of *love:* "I love [not *am loving*] my family very much.")

• The list of nonprogressive (i.e., stative) verbs is by no means complete. For the most part, it stresses only those verbs used in the exercises. A few other verbs you may or may not wish to mention as being nonprogressive when used to describe "states" are *amaze, astonish, concern, equal, exist, impress, involve, lack, measure, please, regret, resemble, satisfy, sound, surprise, wish.*

◇ **WORKBOOK:** Practice 5.

EXERCISE 12, p. 14. *Nonprogressive verbs.*

TECHNIQUE: *Fill-in-the-blanks.*

ANSWERS: **2.** doesn't belong   **3.** It's beginning . . . don't have . . . is wearing   **4.** don't own . . . wear [habitual activity]   **5.** I'm looking . . . is writing . . . is biting . . . is scratching . . . is staring . . . seems . . . is thinking . . . . What do you think Ahmed is doing?   **6.** is fixing [i.e., repairing] . . . needs   **7.** often tutors . . . is helping . . . doesn't understand . . . are working/ have been working   **8.** am looking . . . looks . . . has . . . isn't having   **9.** is standing . . . Are you talking about the woman who is wearing . . . ? I'm not talking about her. I mean . . . is wearing . . . I don't know. I don't recognize her.   **10.** A: . . . What do you hear? What am I doing? B: I believe you are rubbing . . . . A: . . . Are you listening carefully? B: Aha! You're rubbing . . . . [Follow item 10 with a game in which students close their eyes and make guesses about noises. Have one or several students close their eyes while another student makes a noise of some kind, e.g., writing on the chalkboard, tapping a foot, opening/closing a window or door, closing a book, snapping fingers, blowing, etc. Keep the focus of the game on the use of the present progressive.]

---

* See the INTRODUCTION, pp. xv–xvi, for several suggestions for handling a fill-in-the-blanks exercise.

☐ **EXERCISE 13, p. 16.** *Using present tenses for description.*

> TECHNIQUE: *Written homework.*
> To introduce this assignment, have the class brainstorm ideas for a sample composition that might begin with "I am sitting in my English class" as a way of explaining to them what you want them to write at home.

◇ **WORKBOOK:** Practice 6.

CHART 1-10: USING THE PRESENT PROGRESSIVE WITH *ALWAYS*

• Note the word order for the students: *always* occurs immediately before the main verb.

• The structure in this chart may not be especially significant in a student's overall language usage ability, but it's fun and can be used to point out that a grammatical form can, in and of itself, convey a speaker's emotional attitude. This chart and the following exercise are also good places for students to practice conveying emotion in speech through sentence stress and intonation.

☐ **EXERCISE 14, p. 16.** *Using* always *with the present progressive.*

> TECHNIQUE: *Transformation; teacher-led, oral.*
> Encourage the students to be a bit theatrical as they produce their sentences. Model some of the sentences for the students: say the sentences with annoyance or disgust in your voice, emphasizing the word *always*. Use some gesture of annoyance such as rolling your eyes upward and lifting your eyebrows while saying *always*, or making some forceful gesture with your hands and arms. Students should repeat your sentence with the same voice and gestures. In some sentences, use *constantly* or *forever* instead of *always* for variation.
> Item 8 is a dialogue for completion. (See the INTRODUCTION for ways of handling completion exercises.) Encourage the students to use voice and gestures to show annoyance.

◇ **WORKBOOK:** Practice 7.

CHART 1-11: REGULAR AND IRREGULAR VERBS

• Review the terminology.

• The list on pp. 18–19 is for reference. Ask the students to look through it to see if they have any questions about vocabulary or pronunciation. Define and pronounce as necessary.

◇ **WORKBOOK:** Practice 8.

☐ **EXERCISE 15, p. 20.** *Pronunciation of -ed.*

> TECHNIQUE: *Oral, teacher-led.*
> For items 1 through 24, students repeat after you. Discuss the difference between voiceless and voiced sounds. (The voiceless sounds in English are the consonants /p t k h f Θ s č š/. Other consonants and all vowels are voiced.) To explain voiced vs. voiceless sounds, have the students put their hands to their throats so they can feel their voice box vibrate when they make the /v/

sound but not when they make the /f/ sound. Point out that their teeth and lips are in exactly the same position for both sounds. Other voiceless/voiced pairs that you can similarly demonstrate are /t/ and /d/, /s/ and /z/, /p/ and /b/.

For items 25 through 35, ask a student to read one sentence aloud. You may then ask the student to tell you which pronunciation was attempted for each past tense verb, or ask the rest of the class what they heard.

ALTERNATIVE: *Group work* for items 25 through 35, in which students monitor each other.

ANSWERS: **25.** jumped /pt/, shouted/təd/ **26.** lasted /təd/ **27.** flooded /dəd/, inundated /təd/ **28.** tapped /pt/ **29.** described /bd/ **30.** demanded /dəd/ **31.** departed/ təd/, landed /dəd/ **32.** pushed /št/, pulled /ld/ **33.** handed /dəd/ **34.** tooted /təd/ **35.** asked /kt/

☐ **EXERCISES 16 → 19, pp. 20-23.** *Review of simple past of irregular verbs.*

TECHNIQUE: *Oral (books closed), teacher-led.*

The exercises should go at a fast pace, almost like a game. Responses can be individual or the whole class together. Students should be encouraged to respond as quickly as possible rather than to formulate their answers in their mind's eye first. A mistake is nothing more than a learning opportunity. Tell them just to open their mouths and see what happens. (This encouragement is especially pertinent for those cultural groups that tend to write what they want to say in their minds before they speak and judge themselves harshly if they err.) They may be surprised by how much they already know. And while they're practicing irregular verbs, they're also building fluency.

ALTERNATIVE: *Group work.* After you set the pace and demonstrate the format, the students can continue in small groups with leaders asking the questions. Only the leaders have their texts open. The leaders are responsible for monitoring the responses.

Exercises 16 → 19 can be done over several class periods, not all at one time. They can also be repeated at a later time, after a few days or weeks, for review. They are good for the last five minutes of a class period. They can also be used as oral test items.

SUGGESTION: If you wish, include some regular verbs: Did you *wait* for the bus this morning? Did you *watch* TV last night? Did you *open* the window? etc.

EX. 16 ANSWERS: **1.** Yes, I drank some coffee before class. **2.** Yes, I brought my books to class. **3.** . . . forgot my . . . . **4.** shook **5.** caught **6.** drove **7.** lost **8.** found **9.** wound **10.** . . . understood what you said. **11.** . . . told my friend . . . . **12.** spread [no change in form] **13.** fell **14.** hurt [no change in form] myself **15.** flew **16.** wore **17.** hung **18.** ate **19.** took **20.** rode **21.** swore to tell [This refers to a formal promise, as in a court of law.] **22.** Yes, I forgave you. **23.** wrote **24.** No! The dog bit me! [a little humor!]

EX. 17 ANSWERS: **1.** No, someone else made a mistake. **2.** broke **3.** stole **4.** took **5.** drew **6.** swept **7.** taught **8.** dug **9.** fed **10.** hid your book from you. **11.** blew **12.** threw **13.** tore **14.** built **15.** spoke to [Add a person's name in the blank space.]

EX. 18 ANSWERS: **1.** Yes, I gave you some money. **2.** stood **3.** chose [Comment on the spelling and pronunciation of *choose* and *chose*.] **4.** ran [If the class does not meet in the morning, substitute another time word.] **5.** slept **6.** heard **7.** withdrew **8.** woke up [*Waked* is also possible.] **9.** swam **10.** went **11.** bent **12.** sent **13.** sang [Be sure the pronunciations of *sang* and *song* are different.] **14.** stuck **15.** ground **16.** struck **17.** lit [*Lighted* is also acceptable.] **18.** meant **19.** held **20.** spoke to [Add someone's name.]

EX. 19 ANSWERS: **1.** Yes, class began at . . . [Add the correct time.] **2.** rose **3.** cut [no change in form] **4.** bled **5.** grew **6.** stung **7.** rang **8.** froze **9.** quit [no change in form; *quitted* also possible in British English] **10.** fought **11.** crept **12.** shot **13.** fled **14.** won **15.** slid **16.** swung **17.** blew up **18.** burst [no change in form] **19.** broadcast [no change in form] **20.** knew

◇ **WORKBOOK:** Practices 9 through 13.

☐ **EXERCISE 20, p. 23.** *Special attention in a few troublesome verbs.*

TECHNIQUE: *Discussion; seatwork.*
        Discuss the chart. (If necessary, refer students to Appendix 1, Unit A-1, for further information about transitive and intransitive verbs.) Then do the exercise entries as brief seatwork, followed by discussion of correct answers.

ANSWERS: **1.** raised   **2.** rises   **3.** sat   **4.** set   **5.** lay   **6.** lying   **7.** laid   **8.** lie   **9.** lies   **10.** hung.

◇ **WORKBOOK:** Practice 14.

CHARTS 1-12 and 1-13: SIMPLE PAST AND PAST PROGRESSIVE

• Suggestion: In your presentation, compare the tenses in some of the example sentences with other tenses. For example:
        *I **stood** under a tree when it **began** to rain.* vs. *I **was standing** under a tree when it **began** to rain.* vs. *I **had stood** under a tree when it **began** to rain.* vs. *I **had been standing** under a tree for several minutes when it **began** to rain.* vs. *I **will stand** under a tree when it **begins** to rain.* vs. *I **will be standing** under a tree when it **begins** to rain.* [Demonstrate these various relationships by using an imaginary tree and rain.]

• This chart is the first place the word ''clause'' is mentioned. You may wish at this point to explain that a clause is a structure that has a subject and a verb, and make the distinction between a main (independent) clause and a dependent clause. Students will concentrate on complex sentences in later chapters. Adverb clauses of time are in Chapter 8. You may wish to refer the students to Charts 8-4 and 8-5, but at this point it is usually sufficient simply to refer to ''*when* clauses'' and ''*while* clauses.'' The text assumes that the students are quite familiar with sentences containing basic adverb clauses of time with subordinating conjunctions such as *when, while, before,* and *after.* For the time being, keep the focus on verb tenses, with minimal attention to complex sentence structure.

• Note in (i) and (j): In sentences with *when,* the progressive usually occurs in the main clause. In sentences with *while,* the progressive usually occurs in the ''*while* clause.'' (Sometimes *when* has the same meaning as *while,* and the progressive is used in a ''*when* clause'':e.g., *When [i.e., while] I was walking home last night, I suddenly remembered that it was my wife's birthday.*)

☐ **EXERCISES 21 & 22, pp. 24–27.** *Simple past vs. past progressive.*

TECHNIQUE: *Fill-in-the-blanks.*
        Exercises 21 and 22 are similar. One can be done in class and the other assigned for out-of-class preparation for the next class.
        In Exercise 22, some items are dialogues between Speakers A and B. Two students can read a dialogue aloud. Then you can ask them to repeat it with their books closed. This is a good technique to use occasionally for improving fluency.

EX. 21 ANSWERS: **2.** didn't want to . . . was raining   **3.** called . . . wasn't . . . was studying   **4.** did not hear . . . was sleeping   **5.** was shining . . . was blowing . . . were singing   **6.** were arguing . . . walked   **7.** opened . . . found   **8.** were not . . . were playing   **9.** was climbing . . . tripped . . . fell . . . didn't hurt   **10.** was reading . . . fell . . . closed . . . tiptoed   **11.** was snowing . . . was shining . . . were shoveling [also spelled: shovelling] . . . was lying   **12.** was shoveling [shovelling] . . . brought

EX. 22 ANSWERS: **1.** almost had . . . was driving . . . saw . . . was coming . . . stepped . . . swerved . . . just missed   **2.** decided . . . were starving   **3.** finally found . . . was already . . .

were talking busily/were busily talking . . . were speaking . . . were conversing . . . were just sitting . . . chose . . . sat . . . walked . . . stopped   **4.** A: Did you hear . . .   B: wasn't listening . . . was thinking   **5.** B: was waiting   **6.** B. was she wearing   **7.** B: stepped . . . was running . . . stung   **8.** A: Did you break . . .   B: slipped . . . was crossing

---

CHART 1-14: USING EXPRESSIONS OF PLACE WITH PROGRESSIVE TENSES

• The point is that prepositional phrases of place can have two positions: (1) the neutral position at the end of the clause or (2) the focus position, which emphasizes the place, between *be* and the main verb.

• The neutral position is used in answer to "What?" questions because the focus is then on the activity. The focus position is used in answer to "Where?" questions.

☐ **EXERCISE 23, p. 27.** *Expressions of place with progressive verbs.*

TECHNIQUE: *Transformation; teacher-led, oral.*

Items 1 through 5 require only a change in position. You or a student can read the sentence, then another student can say the changed sentence. Or a student can simply give the transformation.

For more advanced groups, items 1 through 5 can be given an expanded form. Two or four students can be Speakers A and B or A, B, C, and D.

  1. A: *What's Sally doing?*
     B: *She's listening to music in her room.*
     A or C: *Where's Sally?*
     B or D: *She's in her room, listening to music.*

Items 12 through 16 can be done with books closed. Make the items more interesting by using names of familiar persons in place of the names in the book. Make up additional oral cues by asking questions about familiar persons: Where is (*name of a school administrator*) now, and what is s/he doing? Where were you last night at nine, and what were you doing? etc.

POSSIBLE ANSWERS: **2.** Roy is on the couch taking a nap.   **3.** Anita was in England (last month) attending a concert (last month). [Either position for the expression of time is acceptable.] **4.** The teacher is at her desk . . . .   **5.** . . . because they were at the park playing . . . . **7.** He's upstairs _____ing . . . .   **8.** She's in her office _____ing . . . .   **9.** She's in the kitchen _____ing . . . .   **10.** He was at home _____ing . . . .   **11.** He was in New York _____ing . . . .   **13.** . . . I was in _____ lying in the sun.   **14.** We are _____ studying . . .   **15.** . . . . because he was _____ hiding from . . . .   **16.** . . . she was _____ trying to . . . . [Note that the expression of place cannot come between *was* and *supposed* because that is not a progressive tense form.]

◇ **WORKBOOK:** Practices 15, 16, 17.

☐ **EXERCISE 24, p. 28.** *Describing past activities.*

TECHNIQUE: *Pantomime.*

A pantomime is performed silently. Ideas are communicated by gestures and movements, not by words. Individual students choose incidents to pantomime. They need to think for a while about how they will perform.

Demonstrate a pantomime yourself or select a volunteer. Then ask a student to describe what happened using past verbs. Other students can then add details that were missed. Your task is to focus attention on the correct use of verb tenses because, in the excitement of describing the details, students may tend to slip into present or uninflected forms. The grammar focus should be on consistent use of past verbs. You may wish to let other errors go by unremarked.

ALTERNATIVE: Students can divide into small groups and follow the above steps. A leader in each group can watch the time limit. Tell the students to monitor each other on the use of past verbs.

☐ EXERCISE 25, p. 29. *Using tenses and expressions of time.*

> TECHNIQUE: *Written homework.*
> A written description can be done either before or after an oral description of a pantomime. The writing can be done either in or out of class. Usually the students are able to produce better writing when it follows class discussion of a pantomime.
> ALTERNATIVE: Prior to assigning written homework, write one description as a group activity, with you writing on the chalkboard as students suggest sentences. Then revise the writing with the help of the class and focus the students' attention on chronological organization and the use of "time words" as connective devices.

CHART 1-15: PRESENT PERFECT

• Compare the example sentences with similar sentences in the simple past; e.g., *They have moved into a new apartment* vs. *They moved into a new apartment last week.*

• The use of the present perfect illustrated by examples (i) though (m) carries the same meaning as the present perfect progressive: it expresses the duration of an activity that began in the past and continues to the present. The present perfect is used to express this meaning primarily for nonprogressive, i.e., stative, verbs. With almost all other verbs, the present perfect progressive is used to express duration. In other words, the present perfect is used to express the <u>duration</u> of a "state," but the present perfect progressive is used to express the duration of an "activity." Note that all the verbs in (i) through (m) are nonprogressive.

• Special attention may need to be paid to (e) and (k), where *have* is an auxiliary and *had* is the main verb.

☐ EXERCISE 26, p. 30. *The simple past and present perfect.*

> TECHNIQUE: *Fill-in-the-blanks.*
> Explain phrases like "so far" and "up to now" as necessary.

> ANSWERS: **2.** went **3.** arrived **4.** has been **5.** have already missed . . . missed **6.** saw **7.** has never seen [*Never saw* is also possible. It would mean that either Anna is now dead or you are telling a story about a fictional character who lived in the past.] **8.** have known [*Knew* would mean that "Greg Adams" is, in all likelihood, dead.] **9.** have had **10.** has given

◇ WORKBOOK: Practice 18.

☐ EXERCISE 27, p. 30. *Using the present perfect tense.*

> TECHNIQUE: *Oral (books closed), teacher-led.*
> SUGGESTION: Expand the scope of the exercise by eliciting similar sentences using the simple past: *How many books have you bought since the beginning of the semester?* can be followed by *When did you buy this book?*
> As with any teacher-led oral exercise, omit items irrelevant to your particular class and make up additional items directly related to your students' lives and situations.
> This kind of question-and-answer oral exercise is a good opportunity to get your students talking about themselves. Ask more than one student the same question. Follow up interesting responses by engaging in short dialogues with your students. Questions that you ask

conversationally on the topics suggested in the exercise items can provide the students with excellent oral practice of verb tenses. In addition, you can learn more about your students and they about each other. They may discover, for instance, that others in the class are having trouble meeting people and making friends, or that others miss home cooking and dislike what is offered in the student cafeteria.

☐ **EXERCISE 28, p. 31.** *Using* for *and* since *with the present perfect.*

TECHNIQUE: *Completion.*

One student should read all of the statements for one item, since they are related in meaning.

Frequent problems occur with the word *since*. *Since* may be followed by (1) a specific day or date (*1986, Friday, last January,* etc.) or (2) a clause with a past tense verb (*since I was 12 years old, since he came to this city,* etc.). Point out that it is incorrect to use durational phrases like "since two years" or "since a long time"; in those cases, use *for*.

It is advisable not to encourage the use of time phrases with *ago* following *since* (such as "since three days ago"). Such phrases are sometimes used informally by native speakers, for instance in a short answer, but are likely to be misused by the students at this point. Example of possible informal usage:

A: *You can't drive. You don't have a license.*
B: *Yes I do.*
A: *You do? Since when?*
B: *Since two weeks ago!*

Note: In usual usage, a person would say *I've had my driver's license* **for two weeks** NOT *I've had my driver's license since two weeks ago.*

☐ **EXERCISE 29, p. 31.** *Using the simple past and present perfect.*

TECHNIQUE: *Oral (books closed), teacher-led.*

This exercise should proceed like a natural conversation. You lead it by asking questions. After one student replies, you ask the next student about the first one's response. Therefore, you need to use the names of your students in the blank spaces, and you substitute the name of your city or country in the first line.

Some of your exchanges with students might lead to expansion of the dialogue into a brief conversation. If it seems natural and interesting, keep it going for a minute or two. Students need a break from the routine as well as additional listening and speaking practice.

☐ **EXERCISE 30, p. 32.** *Irregular past participles.*

TECHNIQUE: *Oral (books closed), teacher-led.*

If necessary, remind students that a question with "your" requires an answer with "my," as in items 5, 15, 24, and 28.

In item 17, you should mention the name of someone who is well known in the students' community.

Occasionally, ask students to spell the past participle after they give their answer, especially ones that are frequently troublesome, such as *ridden* and *written*. You might write problem words on the chalkboard.

As always, omit or change items to suit your particular class.

☐ **EXERCISE 31, p. 33.** *Regular and irregular past participles.*

TECHNIQUE: *Oral (books closed), teacher-led.*

You say the cue phrase. (You should substitute appropriate names between parentheses.) Then Student A asks B a question, and B answers truthfully.

You may need to explain that "ever" in a present perfect question means "at least once in your lifetime." It is not used in the answer to a question.

An acceptable alternative to the answer "No, I haven't" is "No, I never have."

If you wish, you may expand some of these short dialogues. After Student B replies "Yes, I have," you might ask when or where the event occurred.

ALTERNATIVE: *Group work or pair work.*

☐ **EXERCISE 32, p. 33.** *Contractions of the auxiliary* have.

TECHNIQUE: *Oral (books open), teacher-led.*

You can either have the students repeat after you, or have the students read the sentences with the contracted forms first and then repeat after you. Make up additional sentences as you and the students wish. (For example, *How long've you been living here? Why's Juan stopped coming to class?*)

It is not necessary for students to use these contractions when they speak, although they are natural for native speakers of English. The main point here is to make the class aware that contractions with nouns and question words exist so that the students might be more likely to hear them when listening to native speakers.

Students often hesitate to use contractions. The result is that their speech sounds stilted and formal in conversations. Comfortable use of contractions comes through experience. You can encourage your students to use contractions but should not require it.

ITEM NOTES: **3.** weather's **4.** neighbors've **5.** teacher's **7.** parents've **8.** [no contraction] **9.** Where've **10.** What've

☐ **EXERCISE 33, p. 34.** *Simple past and present perfect.*

TECHNIQUE: *Fill-in-the-blanks.*

Point out spoken contractions.

ANSWERS: **1.** What have you learned since you came here? . . . have you made . . . have already met **2.** have not had . . . have had **3.** had . . . went [*Last night* signals the simple past; both actions occupied the same time period.] **4.** have gotten/got . . . saw . . . have also gotten/got [*Got* is principally British usage.] **5.** advanced **6.** have made **7.** have changed . . . were . . . have become ["Today" = since the 1800s, still changing.] . . . has also changed . . . were **8.** B: have already taken . . . took **9.** A: Have you ever met . . . B: haven't **10.** have never eaten **11.** [The most common use of the present perfect is without time signals, as illustrated in the first two blanks.] A: have you visited [no time signal] B: I've been [no time signal] A: I've never been . . . were [asking for a specific time signal] B: I've also visited [no time signal—not "two years ago," but a different trip] . . . took ["six years ago"] A: Did you visit [referring to the trip six years ago] A: I've always wanted . . . I haven't had/I've not had . . . went . . . haven't gone

◇ **WORKBOOK:** Practices 20 and 21.

CHART 1-16: PRESENT PERFECT PROGRESSIVE

- Compare the examples with the present progressive.

- Expect students to have difficulty understanding the use of this tense in examples (e), (f), and (g).

☐ **EXERCISE 34, p. 36.** *Present perfect progressive.*

TECHNIQUE: *Fill-in-the-blanks and completion, teacher-led.*

Use items 1 through 3 as additional examples for discussion. Again compare the present perfect progressive with the present progressive.

POSSIBLE ANSWERS: **2.** has been talking **3.** have been trying **5.** It has been raining for several days. Perhaps we'll have a flood. **6.** I've been studying for hours. My eyes are getting tired.   **7.** I've been waiting for half an hour. Did my friend forget our appointment?   **8.** He's been sitting there for twenty minutes. The doctor should be able to see him soon.

☐ **EXERCISE 35, p. 37.**   *Present perfect and present perfect progressive.*

> TECHNIQUE: *Fill-in-the-blanks, teacher-led.*
> ALTERNATIVE: Students can work in pairs or small groups to find the answers. Then the class can review them together and discuss problem items.
>
> *ANSWERS:*   **1.** has been snowing   **2.** have had   **3.** have been studying   **4.** have written   **5.** have been living   **6.** has rung   **7.** has been ringing   **8.** has been playing

☐ **EXERCISE 36, p. 38.**   *Present perfect and present perfect progressive.*

> TECHNIQUE: *Fill-in-the-blanks.*
>
> *ANSWERS:*   **1.** A: Have you been . . . B: I've been trying . . . has been   **2.** A: haven't seen . . . have you been doing   **3.** B: I've never eaten   **4.** A: Have you been crying?   **5.** A: has he been . . . B: . . . has been teaching/has taught

☐ **EXERCISE 37, p. 38.**   *Using* since.

> TECHNIQUE: *Completion.*
> Students may use either the present perfect or the present perfect progressive, or both if you wish.

◇ **WORKBOOK:** Practices 22, 23, 24.

CHARTS 1-17 AND 1-18: PAST PERFECT AND PAST PERFECT PROGRESSIVE

• Compare the examples with similar sentences containing (1) the present perfect and present perfect progressive, and (2) the simple past.

• Point out that <u>two</u> past events or times are necessary in order to use the past perfect. The <u>earlier</u> event uses the past perfect tense. The progressive form may be used to express duration or recentness, as with the present progressive.

• You might anticipate that students sometimes have the erroneous idea that the past perfect is used to express an event that happened a long, long time ago. In the use of the past perfect, <u>when</u> an event occurred in the past is important only in relation to another time or event in the past.

• The expression "by the time" usually needs some explanation. It conveys the idea that one event was or will be completed before another event. It usually signals that either the past perfect (progressive) or the future perfect (progressive) needs to be used in the main clause (and, in fact, is used to signal only those tenses in the exercises in the text—even though it is possible to use other tenses when a "state" rather than an "event" is being expressed: *The doctor came at six. By that time, it* **was** *too late* [state]. *The patient* **was** *dead* [state] *or* **had died** [event].).

• In (b) and (c), the simple past may be used in informal English. In other words, it is sometimes, but by no means always, possible to use the simple past in place of the past perfect. The past perfect is relatively formal; the past perfect progressive is relatively infrequent. Students may find these tenses more useful in written English than in everyday spoken English, with the possible exception of their use in conditional sentences (Chapter 10) and sequence of tenses in noun clauses (Chapter 7).

☐ **EXERCISE 38, p. 40.** *Pronunciation of the auxiliary verb* had.

TECHNIQUE: *Oral, teacher-led.*

ITEM NOTES: [Items 1 and 2 show the contractions with pronouns. Other items require students to supply the spoken contractions.] **3.** "children-/əd/" **4.** "roommates-/əd/" **5.** [No contraction is possible because "had" is the main verb.] **6.** "flood-/əd/" **7.** Where'd [spoken as a single syllable /wɛrd/, but note that "d" before "y" in "you" becomes /ǰ/— "Where-/ǰu/"] **8.** Who'd [hu:d]

☐ **EXERCISES 39 & 40, pp. 40-41.** *The simple past and past perfect.*

TECHNIQUE: *Fill-in-the-blanks.*

EX. 39 ANSWERS: **1.** . . . had been/was [Both are possible because the word "before" shows the relationship between the two events.] . . . became **2.** felt . . . took/had taken [Both are a possible with "after."] **3.** had already given . . . got **4.** left . . . had collected **5.** was . . . had stopped

EX. 40 ANSWERS: **1.** had already begun . . . got . . . quietly took **2.** roamed . . . had become . . . appeared **3.** had never seen [possibly *never saw* in very informal English] . . . visited **4.** had already boarded . . . got **5.** saw . . . had not seen [before I saw her yesterday] . . . did not recognize . . . had lost [before I saw her yesterday]

◇ **WORKBOOK:** Practices 25, 26, 27.

☐ **EXERCISE 41, p. 41.** *The present perfect progressive and past perfect progressive.*

TECHNIQUE: *Fill-in-the-blanks.*

ANSWERS: **1.** have been studying **2.** had been studying **3.** had been daydreaming **4.** have been sleeping **5.** had been standing

◇ **WORKBOOK:** Practice 28.

☐ **EXERCISE 42, p. 42.** *Review of present and past verbs.*

TECHNIQUE: *Discussion of meaning.* ★

ANSWERS: **2.** Gloria [Riding her bicycle was in progress at the time the rain stopped, meaning she began to ride her bike before the rain stopped. Paul rode his bicycle <u>after</u> the rain stopped: the "*when* clause" happens first when both clauses contain the simple past.] **3.** Dick [Ann went to the store after she had run out of food. Dick went to the store while running out of food was in progress.] **4.** Mr. Sanchez ["taught for nine years," simple past, indicates that the activity was completed in the past; "has taught for nine years" means he is still teaching, i.e., the activity is not completed.] **5.** Alice [George walked to the door only after the doorbell rang. Alice knew someone was coming to ring her doorbell because she began to walk toward the door before the bell rang.] **6.** Joe [Maria finished eating before I arrived. Joe ate after I got there, so he was the one who was still hungry.] **7.** Carlos [similar to item 4] **8.** Jane [Sue's lying in the sun was still in progress when she applied lotion.] **9.** Mr. Fox [Mr. Fox's waving was already in progress when I looked across the street.]

★ See the INTRODUCTION, p. xvii, for suggestions for handling discussion-of-meaning exercises.

EXERCISE 43, p. 43. *Past time narrative.*

TECHNIQUE: *Oral (books closed), teacher-led or group work.*
Have the students read the example before they close their books. The stories may get a little silly, but the students should have fun.

☐ **EXERCISE 44, p. 44.** *Past time narrative.*

TECHNIQUE: *Written group work.*
Each person in the group is to begin a story. In a group of six people, six different stories will be circulating at the same time.
A time limit (2–3 minutes per contribution) is advisable unless you wish to make this an activity that takes up an entire class period.
After the stories are written and you are discussing them in class, you may or may not wish to bring up the possibility of using present tenses in a narrative. For example: *Let me tell you about Pierre's day yesterday. He gets in trouble as soon as his alarm clock rings. When he hears the alarm and gets out of bed, he steps on a snake! Would you believe that? He's nearly frightened to death, but the snake slithers away without biting him. Etc.* The text doesn't deal with this use, but you might want to explore it with an advanced class.

◇ **WORKBOOK:** Practice 29.

CHART 1-19: SIMPLE FUTURE/*BE GOING TO*

• This chart merely introduces the two basic forms for expressing the future. It does not show their differences in function or meaning; see Chart 1-20.

• Model "gonna" for the students. Don't rush them to use it in their speech, and remind them that good enunciation is important to second-language learners and that normal contracted speaking will occur naturally as they gain experience with the language. Point out that "gonna" is not used in writing.

☐ **EXERCISE 45, p. 44.** *Pronunciation of contracted* will.

TECHNIQUE: *Oral, teacher-led.*
Contraction of *will* is natural in conversation; this exercise gives students practice in hearing these forms and trying to produce them themselves. Most of the personal pronoun contractions are pronounced as a single syllable: *I'll* /ayl/, *you'll* /yul/, *he'll* /hiyl/, *she'll* /šiyl/, *we'll* /wiyl/, *they'll* /ðeyl/. Other words add a syllable for the contraction: *it'll* /ıtəl/, *that'll* /ðætəl/, etc.

ANSWERS: [Items 1 to 4 show the commonly written contracted forms. In other items, the forms are not usually written but should be spoken in this exercise.]   **6.** weather'll   **7.** Mary'll   **8.** Bill'll   **9.** children'll   **10.** Who'll [This is sometimes a written form, also. It is pronounced as one syllable /hu:l/.]   **11.** Where'll   **12.** long'll   **13.** Nobody'll   **14.** That'll   **15.** What'll

---

CHART 1-20: *WILL VERSUS BE GOING TO*

• Students often ask about the difference between *will* and *be going to* even though in their own independent production they may only rarely make the mistake of using one where the other is required.

□ **EXERCISE 46, p. 46.** Will *and* be going to.

TECHNIQUE: *Fill-in-the-blanks, teacher-led or group work.*

Most of the items are dialogues between Speaker A and Speaker B. Students can work out the answers in small groups, then speak the dialogues in a natural manner. You may wish to encourage them to experiment with contractions when they speak.

ANSWERS: *PART I* [Note that there is no difference in meaning between *will* and *be going to* in these sentences.]   **2.** will be/is going to be . . . will come/is going to come   **3.** B: I'll probably see/I'm probably going to see   **4.** will be/is going to be   **5.** A: will not/won't/is not going to be . . . Who'll be/Who's going to be   B. will/is going to teach . . . I'll/I'm going to be . . . you'll/you're going to be

PART II [Note that there is a difference in meaning here between *will* and *be going to: will* expresses ''willingness'' and *be going to* expresses ''a prior plan.'']   **8.** I'll get   **9.** I'll turn   **10.** A: I'm going to enroll . . . I'm going to take   **11.** B: I'll make . . . That will   **12.** B: I'll get   **13.** B: I'm going to be   **14.** A: I'm going to place   **15.** B/C/D: I'll do it!   **16.** B: I'm going to erase

◇ **WORKBOOK:** Practices 30 and 31.

CHART 1-21: EXPRESSING THE FUTURE IN TIME CLAUSES

• The focus is on verb usage in complex sentences containing dependent (subordinate) adverbial clauses, called ''time clauses'' here. The structure of sentences with these clauses is discussed more thoroughly in Chapter 8.

• Learners naturally feel that it is logical to use the future tense in the time clause as well as in the main clause. Point out that that is not traditional in English usage. There are certain patterns and systems within a language, but a language should not be expected to be completely logical.

□ **EXERCISE 47, p. 48.** *Using future and simple present with time clauses.*

TECHNIQUE: *Fill-in-the-blanks, teacher-led.*

Keep attention focused on the time clause. Problems may occur because students try to use future verbs instead of the simple present there.

In items 7 and 8, the verbs ''plan,'' ''hope,'' and ''intend'' are used. These words refer to a *present* condition, a thought or feeling *at this moment* about a future activity. Therefore, they are in a present, not in a future, tense form. Plans, hopes, and intentions occur in the present but concern future activities.

ANSWERS: **2.** eat [*Have eaten* is also correct, but try to keep the focus on the two choices in the directions: *will/be going to* or the simple present.] . . . will probably take/am probably going to take   **3.** get . . . I'll call/I'm going to call   **4.** watch . . . I'll write/I'm going to write   **5.** I'll wait/I'm going to wait . . . comes   **6.** stops [or *has stopped*] . . . I'll walk/I'm going to walk   **7.** graduate . . . intend [present tense because now it is my plan] . . . will go/am going to go . . . get   **8.** are you going to stay/will you stay . . . plan . . . hope . . . are you going to do/will you do . . . leave . . . I'll return/I'm going to return . . . get [Point out the parallel structure, in which the subject and auxiliary don't need to be repeated after *and*.] I'll be . . . return . . . get

□ **EXERCISE 48, p. 49.** Will/be going to *and the simple present.*

TECHNIQUE: *Oral, teacher-led.*

POSSIBLE ANSWERS: **2.** [simple present . . . future] **3.** [Future . . .simple present] **4.** [future . . . simple present] **5.** [simple present . . . future] **6.** [future . . . simple present] **7.** [simple present . . . future]

◇ **WORKBOOK:** Practices 32, 33, 34.

CHART 1-22: PRESENT PROGRESSIVE/SIMPLE PRESENT FOR FUTURE TIME

• The present progressive, meaning future time, must relate to a plan or intention.

• The simple present, meaning future time, is limited to scheduled events.

• This use of present verbs to mean future time is common, especially in conversational English. The difficulty for students is to learn the limitations of this use.

□ **EXERCISE 49, p. 50.** *Understanding future time and tense relationships.*

TECHNIQUE: *Discussion of meaning, teacher-led or group work.*

ANSWERS: **4.** in the future **5.** in the future **6.** now **7.** in the future **8.** habitually **9.** in the future **10.** in the future **11.** habitually **12.** A: now B: now A: in the future [*Do you want* asks about a present plan for a future activity.] **13.** A: in the future B: in the future **14.** in the future **15.** in the future **16.** in the future **17.** in the future **18.** in the future

---

CHART 1-23: FUTURE PROGRESSIVE

• Relate the examples to similar sentences with the present progressive and past progressive.

• In the exercises in the text, the future progressive is associated with an activity that will be in progress at a specific moment of future time. However, as in (d), the future progressive is also used to express predicted activities that will be in progress at a vague or nonspecific future time: *I'll be seeing you!* OR *I'll be waiting to hear from you.* OR *Just wait. Before you know it, the baby will be talking and walking.*

□ **EXERCISE 50, p. 52.** *Using the future progressive.*

TECHNIQUE: *Fill-in-the-blanks.*

ANSWERS: **1.** will be attending **2.** arrive . . . will be waiting **3.** get . . . will be shining . . . will be singing . . . will still be lying **4.** B: will be lying A: will be thinking **5.** will be staying **6.** will be doing . . . will be attending . . . studying [Point out the ellipsis, the omission of the subject and auxiliary verb, in parallel structure.] **7.** is . . . will probably be raining **8.** will be visiting

◇ **WORKBOOK:** Practice 37.

CHARTS 1-24 and 1-25: FUTURE PERFECT AND FUTURE PERFECT PROGRESSIVE

- These are the two most infrequently used tenses in English.
- Relate these tenses to perfects and perfect progressives in the present and the past.

☐ EXERCISE 51, p. 53. *Future perfect and future perfect progressive.*

TECHNIQUE: *Fill-in-the-blanks.*

ANSWERS: **1.** have been . . . had been . . . will have been **2.** get . . . will already have arrived **3.** got . . . had already arrived **4.** have been sitting . . . had been sitting . . . will have been sitting **5.** will have been driving **6.** will have been living/will have lived **7.** get . . . will have taken **8.** will have been running **9.** will have had . . . dies **10.** will have been

◇ WORKBOOK: Practice 38.

☐ EXERCISE 52, p. 54. *Expressing future time.*

TECHNIQUE: *Oral, teacher-led or group work.*
    Have the students brainstorm ideas about the future. If necessary, ask provocative leading questions. You may wish to have one student ask another a question about a given topic. You may wish to divide the students into groups and just let them talk, with no written or oral reports.
    ALTERNATIVE: Divide the class into small groups. Assign one topic to each group, or allow them to choose a topic. Give them about 10 minutes to develop a presentation of their ideas. Then ask one person in each group to give the information to the class orally.
    ALTERNATIVE: Assign one topic to each student and ask for an oral presentation of ideas. As a followup, students can write their paragraphs and hand them in to you.
    In previous exercises, such as the descriptions of the pantomimes, you have stressed to the students the importance of being consistent in tense usage; for example, if you begin to tell a story in the past tense, stay in the past tense and don't slip into the present. Now, however, point out that a paragraph of sentences on a single topic may *require* a mixing of past, present, and future.

NOTE: The rest of Chapter 1 provides practice with all the verb tenses. When students have to choose the appropriate tense(s) according to context and meaning, it is important that they have opportunities to discuss their choices and understand their difficulties. One of your many roles is to help them become sensitive monitors and effective editors.
    Now that the foundation for verb tense usage has been laid, the students need guided practice and, most important, lots of out-of-class language experiences as the complex process of adult second language acquisition proceeds. You may wish to tell your students that they shouldn't expect to become instant experts in verb tense usage after studying this chapter, but that you expect their development to be excellent and their ultimate goal eminently reachable. (Sometimes students equate second language learning with other academic pursuits. They may feel that once they study a chapter in mathematics or chemistry, they are now masters of the information it contains—and expect the same results in a second language class. You may wish to discuss with your students the many ways in which the study of a second language is different from other courses of study.)

TECHNIQUE: *Discussion of meaning.*

It is not important for the students to name or define the verb tenses. The important lesson is for them to understand and attempt to explain the meaning of each sentence, noting the differences among similar sentences with different verb tenses.

If you have a wall chart or transparency of Chart 1-5, this might be a good time to bring it out again.

ANSWERS:

1. (a) frequently, repeatedly, again and again. (b) at this moment, right now.
2. (a) right now. (b) at this time on a past day. (c) at this time on a future day, or at a specific point of future time.
3. (a) completed before now. (b) completed before another event or time in the past. (c) a plan to complete in the future before another event or time.
4. (a), (b), and (c) have the same meaning. (d) means that the teacher's arrival was a signal for the students to leave immediately. (e) means that the students had started to leave shortly before the teacher arrived, but they had not yet gone.
5. (a) The waiting began two hours ago and is still in progress at present. (b) The waiting began two hours before another event or time in the past. (c) The waiting will have been in progress for two hours by the time another event occurs; the waiting may begin in the future or may have begun in the past.
6. (a) not finished yet. (b) finished at an unspecified time before now. (c) at a specific time in the past (. . . ''last night,'' ''last weekend,'' etc.).
7. (a) in progress recently, but not yet completed. (b) completed, but no date or time is specified.
8. (a) and (b) are the same: You come, then I will begin to study. (c) and (d) are the same: Studying begins before you come and is in progress upon your arrival. (e) Studying will be completed before you come. (f) The studying will have been in progress for two hours by the time another event occurs; the studying may begin in the future or may have begun in the past.
9. (a) completed activity [He probably works in another place now.] (b) present activity that began two years ago.
10. All four sentences mean the same.

TECHNIQUE: *Oral (books closed), teacher-led.*

Approach each item conversationally; add extra words, rephrase the questions, put the questions in relevant contexts. These questions are in the text merely to suggest ideas as you engage the students in an oral review of verb tenses.

In items where there are several related questions, ask a question and wait for the response, then follow that answer with the next question to the same student. Don't stop for corrections or explanations until the item (the conversation) is completed.

Short answers are natural in conversations. However, in this exercise students are practicing verb tenses, so they should answer in complete sentences. Students easily understand that this exercise is a sort of ''grammar game,'' especially an item such as #15.

ALTERNATIVE: This exercise can be done in pairs or small groups. At this point, the students can simply monitor each other and check with you as necessary.

POSSIBLE ANSWERS: **1.** We've been studying verb tenses. We've studied the present perfect tense. We studied it two weeks ago. **2.** We'll have studied adjective clauses, gerunds, and many other grammatical structures. **3.** Yes, I had. [British: Yes, I had done.] We studied some tenses last year. **4.** We'll have been studying it for about three weeks. **5.** I was practicing English. After that, I went to the next class. **6.** I'm answering your question. I've been doing that for about 30 seconds. **7.** I'm probably going to be sitting in this room again. **8.** I'll be sleeping. Last night at midnight I was sleeping. **9.** I'll be living in my own home. I was living in another city.   **10.** I've been to the zoo. I went there last month.   **11.** I eat, study, and listen to the radio.   **12.** Since I came here, I've done a lot of grammar homework.   **13.** I've flown across the Pacific two times, climbed mountains, and written songs. I flew twice last year, climbed in 1986, and wrote a song last month.   **14.** I've given some roses to my mother-in-law.   **15.** [review of all tenses]

☐ **EXERCISE 55, p. 56.** *Review of verb tenses.*

TECHNIQUE: *Fill-in-the-blanks.*

ANSWERS: **1.** is studying [Check the spelling: *yi*] . . . is also taking . . . begin   **2.** had already eaten . . . left . . . always eats . . . goes [Check for *s* endings.] . . . don't usually/usually don't . . . go . . . usually get . . . go [no *will* in the time clause] . . . am going to eat [also possible: *will eat*]   **3.** called . . . was attending   **4.** will be attending   **5.** got . . . was sleeping . . . had been sleeping   **6.** is taking . . . fell . . . has been sleeping   **7.** started . . . has not finished . . . is reading   **8.** has read . . . is reading . . . has been reading . . . intends . . . has read . . . has ever read.   **9.** eats [no *will* in the time clause] . . . is going to go/will go . . . will have eaten . . . goes [no *will* in the time clause]

◇ **WORKBOOK:** Practices 39, 40, 41.

☐ **EXERCISES 56 & 57, pp. 58–59.** *Review of verb tenses.*

TECHNIQUE: *Pair work.*
Make sure the students understand the format.
The main point of this exercise is to practice verb tenses, and the intention is that at least some of the exercise items develop into short natural dialogues between classmates.
You may wish to walk around the room and listen to the exchanges, but don't interrupt. Answer individual questions, but make longer explanations to the class only after the exercise is completed.
A and B should exchange roles for Exercise 57.

☐ **EXERCISE 58, p. 59.** *Using verb tenses in speaking and writing.*

TECHNIQUE: *Pair work.*
When you make this assignment, announce a time limit (perhaps 5 minutes) so that the stories are not long. This is not a dictation exercise, so Student A should listen to Student B's complete story, *then* report it in a written paragraph. Both students should tell their stories to each other first; then they can both write at the same time.

☐ **EXERCISE 59, p. 59.** *Using verb tenses in speech.*

TECHNIQUE: Only a few students each day should speak. Thus, the exercise can continue over several days. Students who are not speaking should be instructed to take notes in order to practice their listening skills. They can note questions to ask for additional information. They can also note problems with verb tenses or pronunciation. These notes can be used for discussion after the speaker is finished.
Remind students of the time limit. During the reports, you may wish to appoint one student as a timekeeper.
As preparation for this exercise, you may wish to bring a newspaper article to class and have the class work together in making a 2–3 minute summary so that the students will understand exactly what you expect. The article may also be used for a discussion of verb forms; you can discuss the verb forms that the students have already studied and point out the forms that they are going to study later (e.g., modals, sequence of tenses in noun clauses, gerunds and infinitives, passives).

□ EXERCISE 60, p. 59.   *Review of verb tenses.*

TECHNIQUE: *Fill-in-the-blanks.*
Students can perform some of these dialogues dramatically, with appropriate gestures and emotional voices. This can be great fun. You might want to assign the dialogues to be memorized by pairs of students and then presented to the class without their looking at their books.

ANSWERS: **1.** I'm listening   **2.** A: Have you met . . . . B: I've never had . . . .   **3.** A: are you doing . . . . B: I'm trying . . . . A: will/are going to electrocute   **4.** A: He's lying . . . . B: see . . . certainly looks   **5.** A: Are you taking . . . ["Econ 120" is the name of a course in the Economics Department.] B: I'm not . . . . A: Have you ever taken . . . B: I have. A: did you take . . . was . . . is he . . . B: is   **6.** B: was yawning . . . flew A: don't believe . . . You're kidding!   **7.** A: . . . went B: I've seen . . . saw . . . It's good, isn't it? [commenting on the general quality of the written work, not on last night's production]   **8.** A: had never been B: were you doing [at that time, last month] A. were driving [Driving to Washington was in progress when A was in B's hometown.]   **9.** A: was . . . haven't received . . . need . . . don't have B: do you need A: I'll pay [indicating willingness rather than a prior plan] . . . get [no *will* in a time clause]   **10.** A: She's not . . . B: I'll be sitting . . . .

□ EXERCISE 61, p. 62.   *Review of verb tenses.*

TECHNIQUE: *Fill-in-the-blanks.*

ANSWERS: **1.** has never flown [*And he has* is a signal that the man is still living, so the present perfect is needed.]   **2.** I've been waiting . . . hasn't arrived   **3.** are . . . reach   **4.** will already have left/will have already left . . . get [time clause]   **5.** are having . . . has been [Upper 90s Fahrenheit = 35°–37° Celsius.]   **6.** went . . . got . . . were dancing . . . were talking . . . was standing . . . had never met [before last night.] . . . introduced   **7.** was lying [possibly *lay*] . . . heard . . . got . . . looked . . . had just backed [*Back into* means to hit something while moving backwards.]   **8.** am planning . . . I'm going to go/I'll go . . . leave [time clause] . . . I'll go/I'm going to go . . . is studying . . . has been living . . . knows . . . has promised [at no specific time in the past] . . . have never been . . . am looking [possibly *look*]   **9.** was sitting . . . got . . . was sitting . . . tried . . . was lecturing . . . had been hiccupping [Also possible: *had hiccupped*; *hiccup* is also spelled *hiccough*.] . . . raised . . . excused   **10.** has been raining . . . has dropped . . . is [Low 40s Fahrenheit = 4°–6° Celsius.] . . . was shining . . . changes . . . wake [time clause] . . . will be snowing

□ EXERCISE 62, p. 64.   *Review of verb tenses.*

TECHNIQUE: *Fill-in-the-blanks.*
Students in pairs can work out the answers. Then one pair can read the whole exercise aloud to the class. Other students should note any errors but should not interrupt the dialogue. At the end, discussion can always clear up the mistakes.

ANSWERS: **(1)** Are you studying . . .   **(2)** Yes, I am. Are you?   **(3)** I've been . . . was studying [possibly *studied*]   **(4)** . . . are you taking   **(5)** I'm taking . . . are you taking   **(6)** I'm studying . . . need . . . take [time clause]   **(7)** have you been   **(8)** I've been . . . arrived . . . I've been studying . . . lived/was living   **(9)** speak . . . Did you study/Had you studied . . . came   **(10)** studied [possibly *had studied*] . . . spent . . . picked . . . was living [possibly *lived*]   **(11)** are . . . came . . . had never studied . . . started   **(12)** do you plan/are you planning   **(13)** I'm not . . . return . . . will have been   **(14)** hope/am hoping

□ EXERCISE 63, p. 65.   *Review of verb tenses.*

TECHNIQUE: *Fill-in-the-blanks.*
ALTERNATIVE: Students in pairs or individually can work out the answers, then write the letter (without the numbers). When they finish, they can exchange letters and look for each other's

mistakes. (Copying from a text is usually more beneficial for lower- or mid-level students than for advanced students, who make few copying mistakes and generally find it busywork.)

This exercise is intended as a model for the student writing in the assignment that follows in Exercise 64.

ANSWERS: **(2)** received   **(3)** have been trying   **(4)** have been   **(5)** have had   **(6)** has been staying   **(7)** have spent/have been spending   **(8-9)** have been   **(10)** went . . . watched   **(12)** have barely had [also possible: *have had barely*, in which case *barely* modifies *enough*]   **(13)** is . . . am sitting   **(14)** have been sitting   **(15)** leaves/will leave/is leaving/is going to leave   **(16)** have decided [possibly *decided*]   **(17)** am writing   **(18)** am getting   **(19)** will take/am going to take . . . get   **(21)** are you getting   **(22)** are your classes going

☐ **EXERCISE 64, p. 66.** *Using verb tenses in writing.*

TECHNIQUE: *Homework. Alternative: seatwork.*

You may wish to require the students to use each of the 12 tense forms at least once. That sometimes results in occasional forced sentences, but the students generally find it challenging and fun.

◇ **WORKBOOK:** Practices 42 and 43.

☐ **EXERCISE 65, p. 66.** *Recognizing errors.*

TECHNIQUE: *Error analysis.* *

Not all of the mistakes are verb tense; some involve capital letters, singular-plural agreement, and pronoun usage. All the mistakes are typical of many learners at this level of proficiency and are the kinds of errors they should be on the alert for in their own writing.

ANSWERS: **1. have been** living . . . **G**rand **A**venue . . . **S**eptember   **2. was** in . . . New York **C**ity [A noun is capitalized when it is part of the name of a particular place.] . . . week**s**   **3. has** changed . . . time**s** [Compare: *city* is not capitalized in this sentence because it is not part of a name.]   **4.** shout**s** . . . make**s**   **5.** when I **arrive**   **6.** ever **told** . . . parents **teach**   **7.** thing**s** . . . appear**ed** . . . want**ed** . . . need**ed**   **8.** I **intend/am intending** . . . when I **finish/ have finished**   **9.** rang . . . **was** doing . . . **dried** . . . answer**ed** . . . I **heard** . . . husband**'s** . . . I **was**   **10.** I **have been** . . . I **have** done . . . thing**s** . . . (have) **seen** . . . places   **11. had** already **hidden** itself   **12. was** writing . . . knock**ed**

◇ **WORKBOOK:** Practice 44. Have students take Practice Test(s).

☐ **EXERCISE 66, p. 67.** *Prepositions of time.*

TECHNIQUE: *Seatwork, fill-in-the-blanks, teacher-led oral.* *

Because these prepositions are related to time, they are presented in this chapter on verb tenses. These prepositions are assumed to be review for the students. General guidelines you might want to point out:

> *in* + *the morning/the afternoon/the evening/(the) summer/(the) fall/(the) winter/(the) spring*
> *at* + *night/noon/midnight/"clock time"/present*
> *in* + *month/year*
> *on* + *day/date*

ANSWERS: **2.** in   **3.** in   **4.** at   **5.** at [also: *about/around*]   **6.** at [also: *about/around/ before/after*]   **7.** on   **8.** in   **9.** in [also: *before/after*]   **10.** on [also: *before/after*]   **11.** on **12.** on [April Fool's Day is always on April 1. It is traditionally a day when people play tricks on each other for amusement.]   **13.** in   **14.** in   **15.** At   **16.** at   **17.** in   **18.** in

---

* See the INTRODUCTION, pp. xiv, for suggestions for handling error analysis exercises and preposition exercises.

Chapter 2: MODAL AUXILIARIES AND SIMILAR EXPRESSIONS

ORDER OF CHAPTER	CHARTS	EXERCISES	WORKBOOK
Form of modals	2-1	Ex. 1	Pr. 1
Polite requests	2-2 → 2-5	Ex. 2 → 6	Pr. 2 → 6
Necessity, prohibition	2-6 → 2-7	Ex. 7 → 9	Pr. 7 → 8
Advisability	2-8 → 2-9	Ex. 10 → 15	Pr. 9 → 11
Expectations: *be supposed to, be to*	2-10	Ex. 16 → 18	Pr. 12 → 13
Cumulative review and practice		Ex. 19 → 20	
Suggestions	2-11 → 2-12	Ex. 21 → 23	Pr. 14 → 15
Degrees of certainty	2-13 → 2-16	Ex. 24 → 33	Pr. 16 → 20, 23
Progressive form of modals	2-17	Ex. 34	Pr. 21 → 22
Used to and *be used to*	2-18	Ex. 35 → 36	Pr. 24 → 25
Would	2-19 → 2-20	Ex. 37 → 39	Pr. 26 → 27
Can/could	2-21 → 2-22	Ex. 40 → 42	Pr. 28
Cumulative review and practice	2-23	Ex. 43 → 46	Pr. 29 → 33 Pr. Tests A & B

General Notes on Chapter 2

• OBJECTIVE: Modal auxiliaries are used in English to express opinions, give advice, and indicate politeness; they express a variety of attitudes. Mistakes with modal auxiliaries can, therefore, sometimes cause bad feelings or misunderstandings between speaker and listener. Students should become aware that sometimes a small change in a modal auxiliary can signal a large difference in attitudes and meanings.

• APPROACH: Students using this textbook are probably already familiar with the most common meanings of the modal auxiliaries. The focus at the beginning of this chapter is on the basic forms, and Exercise 1 calls attention to errors that should be avoided. The rest of the chapter takes a semantic approach, grouping together modals and other expressions that have similar meanings. Matters of pronunciation, spoken/written usages, and formal/informal registers are noted in the charts.

• TERMINOLOGY: The terms "modal auxiliary" and "modal" are both used. Most modal auxiliaries are single words (e.g., *must, should*). Many have synonyms consisting of two- or three-word phrases (e.g., *have to, be supposed to*). No technical term (such as "periphrastic modals") is used for these synonyms in this book, except to call them "similar expressions."

CHART 2-1: INTRODUCTION

• Point out that all the sentences in example (a) express present and/or future time. Students should understand that *could* and *would* express present/future time as used in this chart, but that, in some other situations, it is also possible to use *could* as the past form of *can* and *would* as the past form of *will* (in the sequence of tenses in noun clauses). Students are sometimes not aware that *shall* and *should* are separate modals, not present and past forms of one modal.

• The chart mentions that each modal auxiliary has more than one meaning or use. These are presented in charts and exercises throughout the chapter and summarized in Chart 2-23.

☐ **EXERCISE 1, p. 69.** *Form of modal auxiliaries.*

TECHNIQUE: *In-class discussion.*
　　Ask students to find the error in each sentence and to say the correct form of the sentence. Explain that modal auxiliaries follow rules that affect the form of other verbs in the sentence. If they ask why modal auxiliaries are so different from other verbs, tell them that long centuries of use and change have resulted in these forms; they are traditional in English.

ANSWERS: **1.** She can see it. [no *to*]　　**2.** [no *s* on modal auxiliary *can*]　　**3.** [no *s* on main verb *see*]　　**4.** She can see it. [Modals are immediately followed only by the simple form.]　　**5.** [no *to*]
6. Can you see it? [no *do*; begin questions with the modal]　　**7.** They can't go there. [no *do*; add negation after the modal]

◇ **WORKBOOK:** Practice 1.

CHARTS 2-2 and 2-3: POLITE REQUESTS

• Discuss how polite requests allow the speaker to show respect to the listener. A person who says "Give me your pencil" or "Pass the salt" may seem to be abrupt, aggressive, or unfriendly.

• Point out the levels of politeness and formality in these charts; e.g., a change from *may* to *can* usually signals a slight or subtle difference in the relationship between the people who are conversing.

• The word *please* is frequently used in conversation. This is another way to show respect and friendliness.

• Another typical response to a request, especially in informal American English, is "Okay."

☐ **EXERCISE 2, p. 70.** *Asking and answering polite questions.*

TECHNIQUE: *Oral (books closed).*
　　When you set up each situation for two students to roleplay, add specific details. Set the scene for them. For example, #1: "Olga, you and Anna are having dinner at the Four Seasons Restaurant. You want the butter, but you can't reach it. It's on the table near Anna."
#2: "Frederico, your chemistry class has just ended, and you walk to the front of the lecture hall to talk to your teacher. You want to ask her a question. Yoko, you are the teacher."

POSSIBLE ANSWERS: **1.** A: Could/Would you pass the salt, please? B: Yes, of course. **2.** A: May I ask you something? **3.** (...), may/can I use your phone? **4.** Could you pick me up at the airport next Tuesday at 5? **5.** Can you meet me...? **6.** May I please leave class early today? **7.** Excuse me. May I come in? **8.** Could I see Dr. North later this afternoon? **9.** Would/Could you check the oil (please)? **10.** Excuse me. Could you please explain the formula on page 100? I don't quite understand it. **11.** Hello. May/Can I speak to Mary? **12.** (...), can I see your dictionary for a minute? **13.** Excuse me. Could/Would you please keep an eye on my luggage for a minute? **14.** (...), I have to go to a meeting tonight. Could you possibly tape the six o'clock news for me on your VCR? [VCR = video cassette recorder]

CHART 2-4: POLITE REQUESTS WITH *WOULD YOU MIND*

• An alternative way of asking permission is "Do you mind if I close the window?" Using *would* is a bit more formal or polite than using *do*.

• In casual conversation, the auxiliary and subject pronoun are often omitted and a present—not past—verb is used: "Mind if I sit here?"

• Another informal response is "No. Go ahead," or sometimes even a positive response: "Sure. Go ahead." Both mean "You have my permission to proceed."

☐ **EXERCISE 3, p. 72.** *Verb forms following* would you mind.

TECHNIQUE: *Fill-in-the-blanks, discussion.*

ANSWERS: **1.** ...if I left **2.** repeating **3.** mailing **4.** ...if I stayed **5.** explaining **6.** opening [if the other person opens the window]/if I opened **7.** if I asked **8.** if I smoked [Note: "I'd really rather you didn't" is a polite and indirect way of saying "I don't want you to smoke."] **9.** speaking **10.** changing [if the other person changes the channel]/if I changed

◇ **WORKBOOK:** Practices 2 and 3.

CHART 2-5: USING IMPERATIVE SENTENCES TO MAKE POLITE REQUESTS

• Assumption: Students are already familiar with imperatives. Here, the focus is on softening their effect and making them more polite when they are used to make a request.

• A review of tag questions may be useful. (See Appendix 1, Chart B-4, in the textbook.) Of course, a tag on an imperative always contains the pronoun *you*. Caution: Sometimes a tag on an imperative gives the meaning of impatience or mild anger. For this reason, students should be careful in using a tag question after an imperative.

☐ **EXERCISE 4, p. 73.** *Polite requests.*

TECHNIQUE: *Oral (books closed).*
To make certain the students understand the difference between orders and polite requests, tell them that you are going to give an order or make a rude request that they are then to soften.

26 ☐ *CHAPTER 2, Modal Auxiliaries and Similar Expressions*

Say your cues a little rudely so that the students can clearly discern the difference between what you say and what they say. Point out that often simply adding *please* and changing one's tone of voice can make a big difference.

Say the imperative cue, then allow two or three students to give different forms of the polite requests. Occasionally, have the class imitate your tone of voice for a polite request. Keep the pace moving and lively.

NOTES ON POSSIBLE RESPONSES: In **2, 3,** and **5,** *may I please have* is the most polite request. Other forms may show some impatience or mild anger.

In **10,** note the parallel verbs, which should have the same form in each request: "Please close . . . and turn"/"Would you mind closing . . . and turning."

In **11,** a person typically might say, "Excuse me. Could I get through?" or "Pardon me. May I get through, please?" Point out that a person would never say, "Let me out of the elevator!" unless s/he were panicked or very, very rude. Questions such as "Would you please let me out of the elevator?" or "Would you mind letting me out of the elevator?" show some irritability. Use **11** to point out again how subtle the use of modals can be, and tell the students to keep a sharp ear open for how native speakers make polite requests.

◇ **WORKBOOK:** Practice 4.

☐ **EXERCISE 5, p. 73.** *Using polite requests.*

TECHNIQUE: *Oral (books closed).*

This works best as a teacher-led activity. Use names of class members instead of "your friend" or "a student." Set the scene by adding specific details to the cues. Keep the pace moving, but be sure everyone understands each situation and response. Some of the situations can also be acted out as dialogues between students.

POSSIBLE ANSWERS: **1.** through **15.** [Follow the examples in Exercise 4.] **16.** Excuse me. Could you tell me the time?/Can you tell me what time it is? **17.** Pardon me. Can you show me how to get to the bus station?/Could you tell me where the bus station is? **18.** Hello. Could you tell me what time Flight 62 arrives, please? **19.** Could you please tell me how much this sweater costs? **20.** Excuse me. Can you show/tell me where the library is?/Could you direct me to the library?

☐ **EXERCISE 6, p. 74.** *Using polite requests.*

TECHNIQUE: *Oral/Written.*

Small groups can brainstorm on two or three items, trying to think of as many requests as possible. Two or more groups can work on the same items, then compare their requests.

ADDITIONAL ITEMS: in a bookstore, in a bank, at the post office, in a library, in the headmaster's/professor's office, at a doctor's/dentist's office.

EXPANSION ACTIVITY: Assign your students to write down any requests they hear—polite or not—during the coming week. Also suggest that they write down requests that they themselves make. At the end of the week, use the students' papers for discussion.

◇ **WORKBOOK:** Practices 5 and 6.

CHART 2-6: EXPRESSING NECESSITY: *MUST, HAVE TO, HAVE GOT TO*

• This chart contains information about pronunciation, formal/informal usage, spoken/written forms, and one past form. Students should note and discuss these points.

• Note especially that *must* is used primarily with a forceful meaning. *Have to* and *have got to* are much more frequently used.

• Encourage students to use conversational pronunciations. These are the most natural and frequent forms in spoken English. The phonetic representations of these pronunciations follow:

> *have to* = /hæftə/ OR /hæftu/   *has to* = /hæstə/ OR /hæstu/
> *got to* = /gadə/ OR /gɔtə/

• *Have got to* (necessity) is not the same as *have got* (possession). For example:

> "I've got to get some money." (I need money.)
> "I've got some money." (I have money.)

□ EXERCISE 7, p. 75.   *Pronouncing* have to *and* have got to.

TECHNIQUE: *Oral (books closed).*
   Ask item **1** of the whole class and let several students call out answers. Encourage them to pronounce *have to* as "haftu" or "hafta" and *got to* as "gotta." (One common mistake is to say "I've gotta to go," inserting an additional *to*.)
   Ask the remaining items of individual students, using classmates' names in the blank spaces.

POSSIBLE ANSWERS: **1.** I've/We've got to study tonight.   **2.** He/She has to go to the bookstore.   **3.** I've got to go home and clean my room.   **4.** He's/She's got to meet some friends at the library.   **5.** I really must write a letter to my aunt.   **6.** Yesterday I had to wash my hair.   **7.** Where do you have to go this evening? [In British English, an alternative is "Where have you to go?" But both British and American English more often use *do* in these questions.]

ADDITIONAL ITEMS requiring more imaginative answers:
   a. What colors do you have to mix to produce the color green?
      (yellow + blue = green; yellow + red = orange, etc.)
   b. How did the astronauts prepare for space travel?
      (They had to train physically for weightlessness, had to learn how to fly the spacecraft, had to learn how to operate computers, etc.)
   c. How can you become a successful language learner?
      (You must be willing to take risks; you have to practice and repeat often; you've got to learn from your mistakes, etc.)
   d. How can you become a good soccer player/musician/dancer, etc.?
      (You have to practice, have to get some equipment, etc.)
   e. What are the best ways to maintain good health?
      (You have to eat a balanced diet, have to get plenty of exercise, have to get enough sleep, etc.)

CHART 2-7: LACK OF NECESSITY AND PROHIBITION

• *Need not* (principally British) and *don't need to* are similar in meaning to *don't have to*; *dare not* (principally British) is similar in meaning to *must not*. Like *need not*, *dare not* is followed by the simple form of a verb: *I dare not **ask** him about it.*

☐ **EXERCISE 8, p. 76.** Must not *vs.* do not have to.

TECHNIQUE: *Fill-in-the-blanks.*
Allow time for students to think about the meaning of each item. The context determines which answer is appropriate. Help students understand the situational context of each item, perhaps by means of roleplaying and discussion.

ANSWERS: **3.** don't have to (needn't/don't need to) **4.** doesn't have to (doesn't need to/need not [Note: no *-s* is added to the modal *need*.]) **5.** must not (dare not) **6.** don't have to (needn't/don't need to) **7.** doesn't have to (needn't/doesn't need to) [There may be some disagreements with the truth of this statement, but the grammar is correct!] **8.** must not **9.** don't have to (needn't) **10.** doesn't have to (needn't/doesn't need to) [This item refers to U.S. university rules. Every student chooses a major field of study, but it is not necessary for a first-year student (freshman) to decide.] **11.** don't have to (don't need to) [Bats are mammals that fly at night.] **12.** must not (dare not) **13.** must not (dare not) **14.** must not/dare not [if you feel strongly that tigers should be protected] OR don't have to (need not) [if you feel that we can decide either to protect tigers or to neglect them] **15.** don't have to (needn't)

☐ **EXERCISE 9, p. 77.** Must not *vs.* do not have to.

TECHNIQUE: *Oral (books closed).*
Keep the pace lively, but allow a student to think of a reasonable answer. Then, additional possible answers can be offered by some other students. This could be done in small groups or as written work, but a teacher-led exercise may be preferable.

POSSIBLE ANSWERS: **1.** argue with their parents **2.** pay taxes **3.** exceed the speed limit **4.** renew their licenses every year **5.** come to school on holidays **6.** forget our homework **7. & 8.** [depend on using a familiar name] **9.** spill food on a customer **10.** cook the food, just serve it **11. & 12.** [depend on personal opinions]

◇ **WORKBOOK:** Practices 7 and 8.

CHART 2-8: ADVISABILITY

• Advice or a suggestion is usually friendly. It is often given by one's supervisor, parent, or friend. It is not as forceful as necessity.

• Note the special meaning of *had better*. It is used in giving advice to a peer or a subordinate, but not to a superior.

☐ **EXERCISE 10, p. 78.** *Using* should, ought to, *and* had better.

TECHNIQUE: *Oral.*
This could be led by you or done in pairs, followed by a brief class discussion.

POSSIBLE ANSWERS: **1.** I have a test tomorrow **2.** I have a test tomorrow [Items 1 and 2 convey the same meaning.] **3.** I'll fall behind **4.** I don't have time **5.** I won't have anything to wear tomorrow **6.** go swimming **7.** take an umbrella **8.** you don't, you'll have to pay a fine **9.** you have an early appointment tomorrow **10.** you'll be too tired to do well on the test tomorrow

☐ **EXERCISE 11, p. 79:** *Giving advice.*

TECHNIQUE: *Oral (books closed).*

Keep the pace lively, but give students time to think of a reasonable response. Discuss some additional responses if students mention them.

POSSIBLE ANSWERS: **1.** You ought to look it up in a dictionary. **2.** You'd better eat some hot soup and get some rest. **3.** You should sit near the front. **4.** You'd better put on a sweater/jumper. **5.** You ought to stamp it on the ground a few times. **6.** You should phone home. **7.** You should discuss it with a legal advisor. **8.** You should tell him/her to sleep on his/her stomach. **9.** You'd better enroll in an English course. **10.** You should get more sleep. **11.** You'd better return it to the library right away. **12.** You'd better stop by the grocery store on your way home. **13.** You ought to go to the bank. **14.** You should clean it up tonight. **15.** You'd better get some gas/petrol. **16.** You should see a dentist. **17.** You'd better go home and go to bed. **18.** You should call a travel agent and check on the flight time. **19.** You'd better drink some cold water. / You should blow into a paper bag. [Explore traditional remedies for hiccups with the class.]

☐ **EXERCISE 12, p. 80.** *Meanings of modals.*

TECHNIQUE: *Oral.*

Lead a brief discussion of each pair of sentences so that students understand the contexts and meanings. Small groups of advanced learners could do this with some imagination.

ANSWERS [Sentences with the stronger meaning in each pair]: **1.** b. **2.** b. **3.** a. **4.** a. **5.** b. **6.** a.

◇ **WORKBOOK:** Practices 9 and 10.

☐ **EXERCISE 13, p. 80.** *Using* should *and* must/have to.

TECHNIQUE: *Fill-in-the-blanks.*

Students can write in their answers, then discuss them in small groups or as a class. You should help resolve disagreements.

ANSWERS: **1.** must/has to **2.** should **3.** must/have to [*Must* is a bit more formal, as in a list of rules for students.] **4.** should **5.** must/have to [if it's a requirement] OR should [if it would help my general education] **6.** should **7.** must/have to **8.** should ["I think having goals is helpful."] OR must/has to ["In my opinion, it isn't possible to live a good life if one doesn't have certain goals."] **9.** must/has to **10.** should **11.** must/have to **12.** must/have to/will have to [*Have to* is preferable here because the situation is neither formal nor urgent.] **13.** should **14.** should **15.** must/have to [spoken with enthusiasm and emphasis]

EXPANSION ACTIVITY: In an advanced class, ask the students to go back over Ex. 13 and use either *ought to* or *had better* if possible. Note that *ought to* (but not *had better*) is always an appropriate synonym for *should*. *Had better* falls between *should* and *must/have to* in strength in items 3, 5, 7, 11, 12, 13. *Had better* is not possible in items 1 and 9 because no "bad result" can be inferred in those two sentences.

CHART 2-9: THE PAST FORM OF *SHOULD*

• Sometimes students confuse the past form of modals with the present perfect tense because the **form** of the main verb is the same (*have* + past participle). If students ask about "tense," tell them that "*have* + past participle" here doesn't carry the same meaning as the present perfect tense; it simply indicates past time.

• The information in Chart 2-12 (e), p. 87, says that the past form of *should* is used to give "hindsight advice." You may want to introduce that concept here: We use "should have done something" when we look at the past (i.e., we look at something in hindsight), decide that what was done in the past was a mistake, and agree that it would have been better if the opposite had been done.

• The short answer to a question is "Yes, I should've" (or British "Yes, I should've done"). Note the pronunciation of *should've*, which is exactly like *should + of*. In fact, some people mistakenly spell the contraction as if it were two words: "should of." Also, students should remember to pronounce *should* like *good*, with no sound for the letter *l*.

☐ **EXERCISE 14, p. 81.** *Using the past form of* should.

TECHNIQUE: *Oral.*
    You or a good student can read the situation aloud, then one student can give an opinion about it, using the past form of *should*. The class should discuss anything that is unclear.

POSSIBLE ANSWERS: [Spoken contracted forms are given here.]   **2.** You should've gone (to the meeting).   **3.** She should've gone to (see) the doctor.   **4.** I should've (invited him).   **5.** She shouldn't've sold it.   **6.** He should've read the contract before he signed it. / He shouldn't've signed it without reading it carefully.

☐ **EXERCISE 15, p. 82.** *Using the past form of* should.

TECHNIQUE: *Oral (books closed).*
    You could do three or four of the items with individual students answering and the whole class listening. The rest of the exercise can be done in pairs or small groups; one student reads the item and another responds. If less advanced students have difficulty, they can open their books.

POSSIBLE ANSWERS: [Spoken contracted forms are given here.]   **1.** I should've worn a coat.   **2.** I should've looked it up.   **3.** I should've written (to) him.   **4.** [The idiom *to be broke* means to be without money.] I shouldn't've spent all my money.   **5.** I shouldn't've opened the window.   **6.** I should've gone . . . .   **7.** I should've set . . . .   **8.** I should've gone . . . .   **9.** He should've married her.   **10.** He shouldn't've married her.   **11.** I should've had . . . .   **12.** I should've stopped . . . .   **13.** I shouldn't've gone . . . .   **14.** I should've gone outside/shouldn't've stayed inside . . . .   **15.** I should've bought (her) something else.   **16.** She should've told the truth.   **17.** I shouldn't've eaten so much food/so many hamburgers.   **18.** I should've returned the book sooner.   **19.** I shouldn't've lent/loaned my car to him/her.   **20.** She should've put her purse in a safe place./She shouldn't've fallen asleep.

◇ **WORKBOOK:** Practice 11.

CHART 2-10: EXPECTATIONS: *BE SUPPOSED TO* **AND** *BE TO*

• The important difference between expectations and necessity (Chart 2-6) is that necessity can sometimes originate within oneself. Expectations come from outside, from other people; therefore, *be supposed to* and *be to* are similar to passive verb phrases with no agent. "He is supposed to come" means "He is expected (by someone) to come."

• Similarly, advisability (Chart 2-8) can originate within oneself, as if one's conscience were speaking. But expectations come from other people.

• Another meaning of *be supposed to* is "it is generally believed." For example, "Sugar is supposed to be bad for your teeth." *Be to* cannot be used with this meaning. (If students ask "Why?," just tell them it's traditional in English.)

• The negative form of these modals inserts *not* after *be*: "I'm not supposed to . . . ," "You're not to . . . ," "He isn't/He's not supposed to . . . ," etc.

□ EXERCISE 16, p. 83.   *Be supposed to.*

TECHNIQUE: *Error analysis (oral).*

    The most common errors: a) omitting *be* before *supposed to*, and b) omitting *-d* at the end of *supposed* because it is not clearly pronounced when *to* is the next word. Other errors involve subject-verb agreement and use of the auxiliary *do*.

ANSWERS: **1. is** supposed to   **2.** suppose**d** to   **3.** suppose**d** to   **4.** I**'m** suppose**d** to
5. you **are** not suppose**d** to [Vocabulary note: An "allowance" is a small sum of money that parents give their children every week or month for their own use.]

□ EXERCISE 17, p. 84.   *Using* be to *in stating a rule.*

TECHNIQUE: *Oral.*

    These are common signs that are posted in the United States in public places such as buildings, buses, and streets. You might compare them with some visual signs such as those for NO SMOKING or NO PARKING and ask students to verbalize the rule of behavior that is represented by the symbol.

ANSWERS: **2.** You/We are to keep off/are not to walk on the grass.   **3.** You are not to eat or drink here.   **4.** You are to move to the rear of the bus. [Passengers are to fill the rear section of the bus first.]   **5.** You are not to joke with the inspectors [especially about carrying weapons or bombs!].   **6.** You are not to use the elevator if the building is burning [because the electricity will probably be cut off]. You are to use the stairs.
7. You are not to litter [throw paper or food on the ground] this area.   **8.** If your car moves slowly [perhaps on a hill], you are to move it to the right side of the roadway [so that faster vehicles can pass/overtake on the left]. [In Britain, these positions are opposite.]

□ EXERCISE 18, p. 84.   *Using* be to.

TECHNIQUE: *Oral (books closed).*

    Set up each situation as clearly as possible, using the students' names. Get the students to imagine themselves in the given situation.

ANSWERS: [Answers depend on students' ideas.]

◇ WORKBOOK: Practice 12.

□ EXERCISE 19, p. 85.   *Review of modals.*

TECHNIQUE: *Oral.*

    This exercise compares the modal auxiliaries from Charts 2-6, 2-8, and 2-10. Students may create a context for each item and decide who the speakers are. For example, items 1 to 4 involve people who are riding in an airplane or automobile; they might be father and son, flight attendant and passenger, two business partners, etc. Students decide which sentence is stronger, and they might also discuss its appropriateness for the context they have created. Some statements are too strong between people of equal status and would cause the listener to become angry.

ANSWERS [The more forceful statement in each pair]: **1.** a.   **2.** a.   **3.** a. [*Had better* is strong, but *must* allows no choice.]   **4.** a.   **5.** a.   **6.** b.   **7.** b.   **8.** a. [*Had better* implies a warning.]

□ EXERCISE 20, p. 85.   *Making meaningful sentences with modal auxiliaries.*

TECHNIQUE: *Oral.*

    This could be a written exercise, including stated reasons. Alternatively, it could be used for group work with students discussing their intended meanings.

ANSWERS: [Answers depend on students' ideas.]

◇ WORKBOOK: Practice 13.

CHART 2-11: MAKING SUGGESTIONS

• These three expressions are followed by the simple (i.e., base) form of the main verb. For example: "Let's *be* careful"; "Why don't you *be* more quiet?" (mildly angry); and "Shall I *be* your partner in this game?"

• *Shall* is used only with *I* or *we*. It is not appropriate to ask "Shall he," "Shall you," etc.

• These suggestions are similar to polite requests, but also may include both speaker and listener in the suggested activity.

• In informal British usage, "Don't let's" is a possible alternative form of "Let's not." "Don't let's" is also heard in American English but is generally considered nonstandard.

☐ **EXERCISE 21, p. 86.** *Making suggestions in a dialogue.*

TECHNIQUE: *Oral.*
Give pairs of students 5 minutes or so to make up dialogues. Then have each pair present their conversation. Encourage imagination and drama. Insist on five to ten lines so that the students can build a recognizable context around their suggestions. Some students might want to write their dialogues. (Memory is short in a second language!) But you should then insist that they say them as naturally as possible, not read verbatim from their papers.
The given sentence can appear anywhere in the dialogue. It needn't be the first sentence. The sentence with "Why don't" should follow the given sentence.

◇ WORKBOOK: Practice 14.

CHART 2-12: MAKING SUGGESTIONS: *COULD*

• Make sure the students understand that *could* refers to present or future time here. Sometimes learners mistakenly think of *could* only as "the past tense of *can,*" but *could* has many uses and meanings. (See p. 112 in the textbook for other uses.)

• *Could* is used to make suggestions when there are several good alternatives. It often occurs with *or*: e.g., "You could do this, or you could try that."

☐ **EXERCISE 22, p. 87.** *Understanding* should *and* could.

TECHNIQUE: *Discussion, teacher-led.*
Students read the dialogues aloud, then paraphrase the *should/could* sentences. The purpose of this type of exercise is to give additional examples of the structure for students to discuss and explore.

POSSIBLE ANSWERS: **1.** B: I advise him to see a doctor./My advice is to see a doctor.
2. I'm making several suggestions. **3.** I'm giving definite advice about how to save money.
4. I'm listing several possibilities. **5.** I'm giving hindsight advice. **6.** I'm listing hindsight possibilities.

☐ **EXERCISE 23, p. 88.** *Making suggestions.*

TECHNIQUE: *Oral (books closed).*

This could be done as group work, but it's very effective to have the students give you advice. They usually enjoy feeling like experts for a change!

Elicit from the students two or three suggestions with *could.* Then elicit one response with *should.*

This exercise benefits greatly from the use of names and places that are familiar to the students. Don't feel that you must read every item exactly as it appears in the textbook. You can create a fuller context, change the order of items, and use more natural phrases to make the exercise more meaningful to your students.

◇ **WORKBOOK:** Practice 15.

CHART 2-13: EXPRESSING DEGREES OF CERTAINTY:
PRESENT TIME

- The percentages are, of course, not exact. They show the relative strength of one's certainty.

- Call students' attention to the note about *maybe* and *may be,* as confusing the two is a common written error.

☐ **EXERCISE 24, p. 89.** *Expressing certainty with* must.

TECHNIQUE: *Oral (books closed).*

POSSIBLE ANSWERS: **1.** S/he must be tired. **2.** S/he must have caught a cold. **3.** S/he must be married. **4.** S/he must be (feeling) cold/chilly. [Idiom note: "Goose bumps" or "goose flesh" refers to the small bumps that appear on your skin when you feel cold or afraid.] **5.** S/he must be hungry. **6.** S/he must have an itch. / S/he must have a mosquito bite. **7.** S/he must be nervous. **8.** S/he must still be thirsty. **9.** S/he must be happy. **10.** S/he must be very sad. **11.** The phone must be dead/out of order. **12.** It must serve good food at reasonable prices. **13.** The battery must be dead. **14.** It must be a good film. **15.** It must be about (two) o'clock.

☐ **EXERCISE 25, p. 90.** *Expressing less certainty.*

TECHNIQUE: *Oral (books closed).*

Point out that the answers in this exercise express less certainty than the answers in Exercise 24.

☐ **EXERCISE 26, p. 90.** *Expressing degrees of certainty.*

TECHNIQUE: *Completion.*

ANSWERS: **2.** He must be rich. **3.** He must be crazy. ["A nut" means, in slang, "a crazy/insane person."] **4.** She could/may/might be at a meeting. **5.** You must have the wrong number. [This is a telephone conversation.] **6.** You must be very proud. **7.** You must feel terrible. **8.** . . . it may/might/could fit Jimmy. **9.** You must miss them very much. **10.** She must be about ten (years old).

◇ **WORKBOOK:** Practices 16 and 17.

CHART 2-14: DEGREES OF CERTAINTY: PRESENT TIME NEGATIVE

• The percentages are not exact; they show only relative certainty.

• Note that the percentages in this chart are not simply the opposites of those in Chart 2-13. *Could* indicates less than 50 percent certainty, but *couldn't* indicates 99 percent certainty. Tell your students they are right if they complain that language is not always a logical structure!

☐ **EXERCISES 27 → 29, pp. 93–94.** *Understanding expressions of certainty.*

> TECHNIQUE: *Completion and discussion of meaning, teacher-led oral.*
> In Ex. 27, compare *must not* with simple present verbs (*she must not study* vs. *she doesn't study*). In Ex. 28, compare *can't/couldn't* with simple present verbs (*it couldn't be Mary* vs. *it isn't Mary*). In Ex. 29, elicit from the students probable/possible reasons for the speakers' verb choices. The last item in Ex. 29 can be done in pairs, then performed and compared.

CHART 2-15: DEGREES OF CERTAINTY: PAST TIME

• Note the parallels between the **affirmative** expressions in this chart and in Chart 2-13.

• Then note the parallels between the **negative** expressions here and in Chart 2-14.

• Point out to students that modal auxiliaries are very useful in communicating opinions, emotions, politeness, and many other notions. Other languages may use very different kinds of expressions for these ideas, so English modals can be difficult to learn.

☐ **EXERCISE 30, p. 95.** *Using past expressions of certainty.*

> TECHNIQUE: *Oral (books closed).*
> Take an active role in this exercise, helping each dialogue develop in a fairly natural way:
> a. Say the first line to the class, using the name of a student instead of "Jack."
> b. Wait for several students to give some good guesses.
> c. Then read the "What if" question and wait for new responses.

☐ **EXERCISE 31, p. 96.** *Degrees of certainty in the past.*

> TECHNIQUE: *Teacher-led discussion of meaning.*
> Assign the roles of the speakers to students. Read the situation cue aloud, then ask the students to read their assigned sentences aloud. They should add information to clarify the meaning of the verb form they have used, or simply explain what they mean by their verb choice.
> Situation 2 might seem odd. It refers to a game called "Clue" that is often played in the United States. The players are given clues to a murder mystery, then they try to solve the mystery and identify the criminal. Note for students that the pronunciation of "Colonel" is the same as "kernel." Also in Situation 2, discuss the use of "you know" as a sentence tag. Students should be aware of its existence but cautioned about its overuse. Perhaps you could illustrate its potential for annoying overuse by telling the class a personal experience story and adding "you know" to each sentence you say. ("Yesterday I went downtown, you know. I had to go to the main post office, you know. My mother sent me a package, you know, but, you know, she didn't put on enough postage, you know. So I have to go pick it up, you know.")

□ **EXERCISE 32, p. 96.** *Using forms of* must *to express degree of certainty.*

TECHNIQUE: *Fill-in-the-blanks.*
Assign speaker roles and ask students to present the dialogues without looking at their texts.

ANSWERS: **2.** must not like [It is possible but not usual to contract *must not* when it expresses "degree of certainty"; the contraction *mustn't* more typically signals "prohibition."]
3. must have (must've) been **4.** must be **5.** must have (must've) forgotten. **6.** must not **7.** must have (must've) left **8.** must be **9.** must have (must've) hurt **10.** must mean **11.** must have (must've) been **12.** must have (must've) misunderstood

◇ **WORKBOOK:** Practices 18 and 19.

CHART 2-16: DEGREES OF CERTAINTY: FUTURE TIME

• Of course, no one can be 100 percent sure about future events. But we can make promises with *will* and confident predictions (as in Chart 1-20) using *will*.

• This chart is titled "future time," but for convenience in section (b), the past forms *should have* and *ought to have* are included. Compare *should have* meaning "unfulfilled expectation" with *should have* in Charts 2-9 and 2-12 meaning "hindsight advice." The forms are identical, but the contexts change the meanings.

□ **EXERCISE 33, p. 98.** *Using modals to express certainty.*

TECHNIQUE: *Fill-in-the-blanks.*
Discuss the fine line between *will* and *should/ought to* to express future certainty, as in item 2. (Learners may sometimes sound brasher or more assertive than they intend if they use *will* instead of other "softer" modals.)

ANSWERS: **3.** must [certainty at the present time] **4.** should/ought to OR will [depends on speaker's degree of certainty] **5.** should/ought to **6.** I'll [a promise, a high degree of future certainty] **7.** should/ought to **8.** will **9.** must **10.** She'll OR should/ought to **11.** should/ought to **12.** should/ought to OR will [possibly depending upon the skill and self-confidence of the cook!] **13.** should/ought to **14.** should/ought to **15.** must **16.** must

◇ **WORKBOOK:** Practice 20.

CHART 2-17: PROGRESSIVE FORMS OF MODALS

• You could elicit more examples. Tell the students: "(...) is at home/in the next classroom/in the school office/at the park right now." Then ask them to describe (...)'s possible activities at the present moment.

Use the same situations but in a past context to elicit past progressive modals: what (...) could/may/might have been doing.

• Every progressive form must contain both a form of *be* and a verb + *ing*.

• Point out similarities and differences with other progressive verb forms in Chapter 1:

Chart 1-8: Present Progressive (*is sleeping* vs. *might be sleeping*)
Chart 1-13: Past Progressive (*was sleeping* vs. *might have been sleeping*)

☐ **EXERCISE 34, p. 100.** *Progressive forms of modal auxiliaries.*

        TECHNIQUE: *Fill-in-the-blanks.*

           Call students' attention to the situations, reminding them that the progressive is necessary for actions that are in progress "right now" or were in progress at a specific point in the past.

        ANSWERS: **3.** must be burning   **4.** might/could/may be talking [in both sentences]
    5. must be playing   **6.** might/may/could be staying [in both sentences]   **7.** should/ought to be studying [advisability]   **8.** must be kidding [an idiom meaning "I can't believe what I just heard. I think you are joking." "Hitchhike" means to ask drivers to give you a ride; traditionally, you ask by pointing your thumb in the direction you want to travel.]   **9.** may/might/could have been kidding   **10.** must have been kidding [more certainty]

◇ **WORKBOOK:** Practices 21, 22, and 23.

CHART 2-18: USING *USED TO* AND *BE USED TO*

• Point out that these two phrases look similar but have very different meanings.

• When *be* occurs, *used to* means "be accustomed to."

• The word *to* in *used to* is part of an infinitive phrase, so it must be followed by the simple form of a verb: *used to go, used to be*, etc. However, the word *to* in *be used to* is a preposition, so it must be followed by a noun, pronoun, or gerund: *be used to the weather, be used to it, be used to living*, etc.

• Special note about *be accustomed to*: In American English *to* is a preposition, but in British English *to* may be considered to be part of an infinitive phrase. So, in British English it is possible to say "be accustomed to live in a cold climate."

• Negative forms of *used to*: [These sentences are more often spoken than written.]

    I didn't use to like fish, but I do now.
    I used to not like fish, but now I do./I used not to like fish, but now I do.
    I usedn't to like fish, but now I do. (British English)

• Question form:

    Did you use to play tennis? (Pronunciation is /yus/.)

• The simple verb *use* means "employ as a tool" and is pronounced /yuz/. Compare these statements:

    I use /yuz/ *a pen to write in my notebook.*
    I am used /yust/ *to using* /yuzɪŋ/ *a pen.*
    I used /yust/ *to use* /yuz/ *a pencil, but now I use* /yuz/ *a pen.*
    Yesterday I used /yuzd/ *a pencil because I lost my pen.*

☐ **EXERCISE 35, p. 102.** *Used to vs. be used to.*

        TECHNIQUE: *Fill-in-the-blanks.*

        ANSWERS: **3.** am   **4.** Ø   **5.** Ø   **6.** are   **7.** is   **8.** Ø   **9.** Ø   **10.** Ø   **11.** is
    12. are . . . am

☐ **EXERCISE 36, p. 102.** *Using* used to, be used to, get used to.

        TECHNIQUE: *Oral (books closed); teacher-led or small groups.*
           Some of these items could also be written as homework.

        ANSWERS: [Depend on students' ideas.]

◇ **WORKBOOK:** Practices 24 and 25.

CHART 2-19: USING *WOULD* TO EXPRESS A REPEATED ACTION IN THE PAST

- Compared to *used to*, habitual *would* is somewhat more formal. *Would* is often preferred in writing, whereas *used to* may be preferred in speech.

- Note the important limitation on *would*: it cannot express a situation, only an action.

- This use of *would* is unusual in British English.

☐ **EXERCISE 37, p. 104.** Would *vs.* used to.

    TECHNIQUE: *Fill-in-the-blanks*.

    ANSWERS: **2.** would give   **3.** used to be [a situation]   **4.** used to be . . . would start   **5.** used to be . . . would get . . . would spend . . . would find . . . would gather   **6.** would ask . . . would never let   **7.** would make . . . would put   **8.** would take   **9.** would wake . . . would hike . . . would see   **10.** would be sitting [in progress at that moment] . . . would always smile and say . . . would stand . . . clear [Note that the modal is usually not repeated in a parallel structure after *and*.] ["Clear her throat" means to make a vocal sound in the throat, usually spelled "Ahem."]

◇ **WORKBOOK:** Practice 26.

CHART 2-20: EXPRESSING PREFERENCE: *WOULD RATHER*

- In a question, either the word *or* or the word *than* can follow *would rather*:

    Would you rather eat fruit or candy?
    Would you rather eat fruit than candy?

- In a negative question, only the word *than* is possible for a preference:

    Wouldn't you rather eat fruit than candy?

☐ **EXERCISE 38, p. 106.** *Practicing* would rather *to express preferences.*

    TECHNIQUE: *Oral completion.*
    Encourage students to use contractions in their spoken answers. The contraction *'d* is often difficult to hear and may be difficult to pronounce for some learners. Sometimes students omit it because they don't hear it.

☐ **EXERCISE 39, p. 106.** *Using* would rather.

    TECHNIQUE: *Oral (books closed).*
    [Answers depend on students' preferences.]
    EXPANSION: Try a round-robin sequence like this:
        Teacher to A: *What would you rather do than go to class?*
        Student A: *I'd rather go bowling than go to class.*

Teacher to B: *What would you rather do than go bowling?*
Student B: *I'd rather play chess than go bowling.*
Teacher to C: *What would you rather do than play chess?*
etc.

◇ **WORKBOOK:** Practice 27.

CHART 2-21: USING *CAN* AND *BE ABLE TO*

• An additional common use of *can* is with stative verbs of sense perceptions [see Chart 1-9 (4), p. 13] that are not used in progressive tenses. For example:

I can smell bread baking in the oven right now. ("I'm smelling bread" is incorrect.)
I can't hear (right now) the lecture. ("I am not hearing" and "I don't hear" are incorrect.)

• Pronunciation notes:

Can't has two acceptable pronunciations. Most Americans say /kænt/. But along the northern Atlantic coast, the pronunciation is similar to the British /kant/.

Can also has two pronunciations. Before a verb, it is usually /kən/. In a short answer ("Yes, I can."), it is /kæn/.

In typical intonation, *can't* is stressed and *can* is unstressed.

☐ **EXERCISE 40, p. 107.** *Pronunciation of* can *and* can't.

TECHNIQUE: You should read the sentences aloud, choosing *can* or *can't* at random. Then ask the students to tell you what you said.

☐ **EXERCISE 41, p. 108.** *Using* can *and other modals.*

TECHNIQUE: *Teacher-led discussion or group work.*

ANSWERS: [Answers depend on students' ideas; some possibilities are listed below.]
1. physical abilities: *can walk, talk, lift my pen;* negative: *can't fly*
2. acquired abilities: *can write, read, play tennis;* negative: *can't speak Swahili*
3. [depend on students' ideas]
4. a. *can walk, can ride my bike, can take a bus.* [possible because certain conditions exist]
   b. *may walk, may ride my bike, may take a bus.* [less than 50 percent certainty]
5. [both give permission, but a. = informal situation; b. = formal situation]
6. [depend on students' ideas]
7. a. *may* expresses idea of "maybe" [less than 50 percent certainty]
   b. *can* expresses idea that "certain conditions exist, so I can choose to do it if I want to"
   c. *will* expresses a prediction or plan
8. [possibly assign to pairs for dialogue construction]

CHART 2-22: PAST ABILITY: *COULD*

• The focus of this chart is the common mistake noted in (c).

• An additional alternative in (d) is *succeed in*: "They succeeded in reaching the top yesterday."

TECHNIQUE: *Oral, discussion; teacher-led.*
This exercise can be confusing.* Focus the students' attention on two points: (1) NOT using *could* to express a single past event that occurred at one particular time in the past; and (2) using *could* to express ability in the affirmative ONLY when it expresses the idea of "used to be able to."

ANSWERS: **4.** could watch [used to be able to]   **5.** could type [used to be able to]
8. could catch [used to be able to]   **10.** could convince [used to be able to]   (All other items contain a single past event, no *could*.)

◇ **WORKBOOK:** Practice 28.

CHART 2-23: SUMMARY CHART OF MODALS AND SIMILAR EXPRESSIONS

• By the time the students reach this chart, they should be familiar with its contents. It summarizes for them what they have been learning in the past 42 pages of the text.

□ **EXERCISE 43, p. 112.** *Differences between modal auxiliaries.*

TECHNIQUE: *Discussion of meaning.*
Ask leading questions to elicit student interpretations of meaning. In addition to a review of grammar, this kind of exercise provides the students with the opportunity to develop their oral skills by explaining something they already know and understand. It challenges them to express their understandings in spoken English. Encourage them to invent possible contexts as a way of explaining differences in meaning.
In some items there is no difference in meaning; in other items there are distinct differences in meaning. In still other items, there might be a subtle difference in politeness or in forcefulness. All of the sentences in this exercise are grammatically correct.

ANSWERS:
1. a and b = a little more polite/formal than c; c = might be spoken to a friend/family member
2. a and b = advisability   c = expected to   d = no choice
3. a = advisability   b = stronger than a; implies a bad result   c = stronger than a or b
4. a = prohibition   b = lack of necessity
5. a = 100 percent   b = 90 percent
6. a, b, c = the same   d = 95 percent
7. a = a guess, 50-50   b and c = 99 percent certain
8. a = maybe he went home, 50-50   b = 95 percent certain   c = a fact, necessity
9. a = advisability   b and c = essentially the same, no choice
10. a = suggesting one possibility   b = giving definite advice
11. a, b = necessity   c = advisability   d = expected   e = possible bad result
   f = preference
12. a = "hindsight advice"   b = "hindsight possibility"
13. a and b = same, repeated action in past

---

*The modal *could* can be confusing. It has many uses, most of which are close in meaning. For example, compare the following:
   I could run fast if I wanted to. [present/future contrary-to-fact conditional]
   I could run fast when I was young. [past ability]
   I could run or I could walk. [50-50 possibility, present/future]
   You could run to improve your physical condition. [present/future suggestion]
Don't be surprised if the students have difficulty with it!

TECHNIQUE: *Fill-in-the-blanks.*

The students have to think of only one possible answer, not all of the possibilities. In the following section, the most likely answers are given first and others are in parentheses.

EX. 44 ANSWERS:
 1. had better shut (should/ought to/have to/must shut)
 2. could/would you hand (can/will you hand)
 3. had to pay...should have returned
 4. don't/won't have to go
 5. May/Could I make (Can I make)
 6. had better take (should/ought to take)
 7. can already say (is already able to say)
 8. mustn't tell (shouldn't/had better not/can't tell)
 9. Could/Would you please repeat (Would you mind repeating)
10. must/have to attend
11. could run (was able to/would run)...can't run
12. had to wait
13. could go
14. would rather go
15. must not have seen
16. can cook
17. had better clean (should/ought to/must/have to clean)
18. can't/couldn't be...may/might/could belong (must belong)
19. would do (used to do)
20. should/ought to/had better/have to/must learn...can be

EX. 45 ANSWERS:
 1. should/ought to/had better get (has to/must get)
 2. can't keep...had better go (should/ought to/have to go)
 3. cannot go (must not go)
 4. shouldn't have laughed
 5. Could/Can/Would you cash
 6. shouldn't stick (oughtn't [to] stick) [Idiom: "stick one's nose in other people's business" means to meddle, to become involved where one is not wanted.]
 7. can't live...have to/must find (had better find)
 8. May/Can/Could I speak...can't come...May (/Can/Could) I take
 9. have to go/have got to go
10. should/ought to take (could take)...can get
11. had to study...should have come
12. don't have to make (shouldn't make)
13. had better answer (should/ought to/have to answer)...might/could/may be
14. must have passed
15. should have been/was supposed to be
16. could/might/may be
17. must have been daydreaming
18. was able to wake (managed to wake) [*Awaken* can also be used instead of *wake*.]
19. would rather have stayed home and watched/should have stayed home and watched
20. could/might/may have been...should have asked (could have asked)

◇ **WORKBOOK:** Practices 29, 30, 31, 32, and 33.

☐ **EXERCISE 46, p. 118.** *Recognizing errors with modals.*

TECHNIQUE: *Error analysis.*

ANSWERS:
1. If you have a car, you ***can travel*** around the United States. (OR If you ***had*** a car, you ***could travel*** . . . .)
2. During class the students ***must sit*** quietly. When the students have questions, they ***must raise*** their hands. [no ***to***]
3. When you send for the brochure, you should ***include*** a self-addressed, stamped envelope. OR When you ***sent*** for the brochure, you ***should have included*** a . . . .
4. A film director must ***have*** control over every aspect of a movie.
5. When I was a child, I ***could go*** to the roof of my house and ***see*** all the other houses and streets.
6. While I was working in the fields, my son would ***bring*** me oranges or candy.
7. I ***broke*** my leg in a soccer game three months ago. [one time in the past]
8. ***Would/Could/Can*** you please help me with this? [***May*** is used with ***I/we***.]
9. Many students would rather ***study*** [no ***to***] on their own than ***go*** to classes.
10. We ***are*** supposed to bring our books to class every day.

◇ **WORKBOOK:** Have students take Practice Test A and/or B.

☐ **EXERCISES 47 & 48, pp. 118–119.** *Using prepositions and phrasal verbs.*

TECHNIQUE: *Seatwork, fill-in-the-blanks, teacher-led oral.*

EX. 47 ANSWERS: **2.** of **3.** out/off **4.** up **5.** at **6.** from [so they couldn't find it] **7.** with **8.** in [arrive ***in*** a country or city] **9.** at [arrive ***at*** a specific building] **10.** from **11.** for **12.** of **13.** at/with **14.** with **15.** to

EX. 48 ANSWERS: **2.** away/out **3.** out/off **4.** up **5.** off [A "raincheck" is a ticket that admits you to the theater another time without additional payment.] **6.** up **7.** out [from a library; "I.D." is an abbreviation for i̲dentification card.] **8.** about **9.** up **10.** back . . . out of

Chapter 3: THE PASSIVE

ORDER OF CHAPTER	CHARTS	EXERCISES	WORKBOOK
Forming the passive	3-1	Ex. 1 → 3	Pr. 1 → 6
Using the passive and "*by* phrase"	3-2	Ex. 4 → 5	Pr. 7 → 8
Indirect objects as passive subjects	3-3	Ex. 6	Pr. 9
Cumulative review and practice		Ex. 7 → 10	Pr. 10 → 13
Passive form of modals	3-4	Ex. 11 → 12	Pr. 14 → 16
Cumulative review and practice		Ex. 13	
Stative passive	3-5	Ex. 14 → 16	Pr. 17 → 21
The passive with *get*	3-6	Ex. 17 → 19	Pr. 22 → 23
Cumulative review and practice		Ex. 20	
Participial adjectives	3-7	Ex. 21 → 24	Pr. 24 → 26
Cumulative review and practice		Ex. 25 → 26	Pr. 27 → 29 Pr. Tests A & B

General Notes on Chapter 3

• OBJECTIVE: In speaking and writing, about one sentence in eight uses the passive structure. In scientific, academic, and informative reporting, usage increases to about one passive in every three sentences. The passive allows one to focus on actions and the receivers of actions, but it does not require identification of the actor because often it is not important or necessary to know who did something. Therefore, the passive is a useful structure for learners to understand and use. However, they should be encouraged to continue using active sentences for direct, forceful, or persuasive purposes when the agent/actor is known.

• APPROACH: Students are given plenty of practice in forming and using passive sentences throughout the chapter. Special attention is given to passive modals, the verb *get* as a passivizer, and the often confusing participial adjectives (*interesting* vs. *interested*). With the charts and exercises, students learn to use various tenses with the passive and to decide whether to use the passive or active form.

• TERMINOLOGY: It is assumed that students understand the grammatical terms "subject," "object," and "(in)transitive verb." The term "*by* phrase" is used for the prepositional phrase that includes the agent of the verb's action.

CHART 3-1: FORMING THE PASSIVE

• Students must understand the difference between transitive and intransitive verbs; refer them to Appendix 1, Chart A-1. Some other languages use transitivity in very different ways, leading students to make mistakes in English (INCORRECT: "The accident was happened" or "My shoe was fallen off").

• In reviewing the tense forms listed at the bottom of the chart, you might have students change some of the statements into questions or negatives. This focuses their attention on the required use of the auxiliary *be* in every passive sentence.

☐ EXERCISE 1, p. 121.   *Forms of* be *in the passive.*

TECHNIQUE: *Transformation, seatwork.* [See the INTRODUCTION to this *Guide* for information about classroom techniques.]

ANSWERS: **2.** is being   **3.** has been   **4.** was   **5.** was being   **6.** had been   **7.** will be   **8.** is going to be   **9.** will have been

EXPANSION ACTIVITY: Before or after Exercise 1, you might want to demonstrate the passive in all the tenses. Ask a student to assist you, then include his or her actions in your sentences. For example: (*"John" touches your book, then takes his hand from it.*)
    TEACHER: John touched the book.
    STUDENTS: The book was touched by John.
    (*You touch the book with your hand and do not take your hand from it.*)
    TEACHER: I am touching the book.
    STUDENTS: The book is being touched by you.
    (*Continue with sentences like the following:*)
    (*simple present*) Mr. Lee touches the book during class each day.
    (*simple past*) When we started this lesson, Baiwong touched the book.
    (*present perfect*) Ruth hasn't touched the book yet.
    (*past progressive*) A few minutes ago, John was touching the book.
    (*past perfect*) Before I touched the book, John had touched it.
    (*future*) Kevin will probably touch the book next.
    (*future*) Pierre is going to touch the book when I ask him to.
    (*future perfect*) Soon Maria will have touched the book.

◇ WORKBOOK: Practices 1 and 2.

☐ EXERCISE 2, p. 121.   *Changing active to passive.*

ASSUMPTIONS: Students can form negatives and questions.

TECHNIQUE: *Transformation, seatwork followed by discussion.*
    This exercise may be done individually or in small groups. In an advanced class where this is review only, a "student-teacher" could lead the exercise.
    Every sentence in this exercise should include a "*by* phrase" in the passive form. Focus attention on the <u>forms</u> at this point in the chapter. Check the students' pronunciation of *-ed* endings.

ANSWERS:
  2. Ann will be invited to the party by Bill.
  3. That report is being prepared by Alex.
  4. Customers are served by waitresses and waiters.
  5. The lesson is going to be explained by the teacher.
  6. A new idea has been suggested by Shirley.

7. The farmer's wagon was being pulled by two horses.
8. The book had been returned (by Kathy) to the library (by Kathy). [Either position is acceptable.]
9. By . . . , the announcement will have been made by the president.
10. That note wasn't written by me. It was written by John.
11. That pie wasn't made by Alice. Was it made by Mrs. French?
12. Is that course taught by Prof. Jackson? I know (that) it isn't taught by Prof. Adams.
13. Those papers haven't been signed (yet) by Mrs. Andrews (yet). [Either position is acceptable.] Have they been signed by Mr. Andrews?
14. Is your house being painted by Mr. Brown?
15. I won't be fooled by his tricks.

◇ WORKBOOK: Practice 3.

☐ EXERCISE 3, p. 122. *Transitive and intransitive verbs.*

TECHNIQUE: *Oral, transformation, with teacher-led discussion.*
The items include intransitive verbs that are often used incorrectly in a passive form by learners (INCORRECT: "My cat was died"; "I am agree with you").

ANSWERS:
3. no change [Compare *died* (intransitive verb) and *is dead* (*be* + adjective).] [Items 3, 4, 7, 9, 11, 12, 13, 15 cannot be passive because they contain intransitive verbs.]
5. That theory was developed by . . . .
6. The cup was dropped by Timmy.
8. I was interviewed by . . . .
10. . . . was destroyed by . . . .
14. . . . , the chalkboard is always erased by . . . .

◇ WORKBOOK: Practices 4, 5, 6.

CHART 3-2: USING THE PASSIVE

• Point out that a combination of factors may determine when the "*by* phrase" is omitted. It is not used:

—when it can easily be assumed who, in general, performs such an action. (*Rice is grown "by farmers." Arithmetic is taught in elementary school "by teachers.*") In such cases, the "*by* phrase" is implied.
—when the speaker doesn't know who performed the action. (*The house was built in 1890 "by some unknown people who engaged in house building." My shoes were made in Italy "by some unknown shoemakers."*)
—when the focus is on the action and it is not important to know who performed the action. (*This olive oil was imported from Spain "by people in a company that imports olive oil."* It's not important to know who those people are. The focus is solely on the origin of the olive oil.)

COMPARE: The active is usually used when the actor is specifically known. (*Mr. Lee grows rice on his farm. Ms. Hill teaches arithmetic in elementary school. My grandfather built our house. The Acme Trading Company imports olive oil from Spain.*)

• The "*by* phrase" is included (in other words, the passive is used even when there is an acceptable active equivalent with a known agent) when the speaker wants to focus attention on the **receiver** of the action (e.g., "this rug" vs. "that rug") rather than on the actor. To illustrate this common use of the passive, as in (f), you might ask two students to draw a simple picture or write a word on the chalkboard. Then you identify the distinction between the two drawings or words by pointing and saying, "This one was drawn/written by (. . .). That one was drawn/written by (. . .)."

□ **EXERCISE 4, p. 123.** *Understanding the use of the passive.*

TECHNIQUE: *Discussion of meaning, teacher-led.*
    You could ask the students some leading questions about the sentences, such as: *Why is the passive used here instead of the active? Who is the actor or agent? Change the sentence to its active form; what's the difference in meaning or forcefulness?*
    ADDITIONAL SUGGESTION: For homework, ask the students to find examples of passive sentences and copy them out to bring to class the next day. Tell them to look in a newspaper, an encyclopedia, a textbook, etc. (This shows them that the passive occurs frequently in many contexts.) At the beginning of the next class, some of the students could write on the chalkboard the sentences they found. Or they could hand in their sentences, which you could then duplicate for further class discussion.

POSSIBLE ANSWERS:
1. We don't know who made the sweater, and it is not important to know. The equivalent active sentence is "Someone (in England) made my sweater (in England)." The passive is preferred here because the actor is unknown and unimportant.
2. The implied "*by* phrase" is "by people who build highways." The passive expresses all the necessary information without the "*by* phrase."
3. "by language teachers," no additional important information
4. It's obvious that the symphony was performed "by the symphony orchestra," not by a high school band or by a guitar player. If the symphony had been performed by any agent other than the obvious one, either the active would be used or the "*by* phrase" would be included.
5. "by television stations"
6. The "*by* phrases" give necessary details. The active forms of these sentences are equally useful. The difference is that the passive focuses attention on two compositions rather than on their authors. Information about the authors is given to identify or distinguish between the two compositions.
7. The "*by* phrase" is used because it contains the important information of "hundreds." The active sentence is equally viable, but the passive focuses attention on the monument.
8. "by people" is uninformative
9. Note that there are four passives here. No "*by* phrases" are necessary. Point out how useful the passive can be when the speaker's/writer's purpose is to give information about the receivers of actions without knowing who performed those actions.
10. The "*by* phrase" is necessary because the agent is known. The active equivalent could be used, but the passive focuses attention on "paper" rather than on "the Chinese." [Items 9 and 10 are related. Even though the active could easily be used in 10, point out that the use of the passive allows a parallel contrast between "parchment" and "paper."]

□ **EXERCISE 5, p. 124.** *Using the passive.*

TECHNIQUE: *Oral; teacher-led or group work.*
    This exercise allows students to apply the rules they have learned so far about the passive: using the correct tense with *be*, omitting or including a "*by* phrase," not using an intransitive verb in the passive, observing singular/plural agreement between subject and verb.

ANSWERS:
3. This antique table was made in 1734.
4. (no change)
5. My purse was stolen.
6. The coffee was being made when .... [The active sentence is perhaps more direct and preferable.]
7. That book has been translated ....
8. That picture was drawn by Jim's daughter. This picture was drawn by my son.

9. The applicants will be judged on . . . .

10. (no change)

11. Is that course being taught by Professor Rivers this semester?

12. When was the radio invented?

13. The mail had already been delivered by the time I . . . .

14. When are the results . . . going to be announced? [Note the plural verb.]

15. After the concert was over, the rock music star was mobbed (outside the theater) by hundreds of fans (outside the theater).

16. . . . because I was told that . . . .

17. The new hospital is going to be built next year. The new elementary school has already been built. [The active sentences with impersonal *they* are acceptable in casual conversation.]

18. If a film is exposed to light while it is being developed, the negatives will be ruined. [The passive makes the sentence more formal and the speaker/writer more distant from the listener/reader.]

◇ **WORKBOOK:** Practices 7 and 8.

CHART 3-3: INDIRECT OBJECTS AS PASSIVE SUBJECTS

• Students may or may not already be familiar with direct vs. indirect objects.

☐ **EXERCISE 6, p. 125.** *Using indirect objects as passive subjects.*

TECHNIQUE: *Oral, transformation, teacher-led.*

You should focus the students' attention on indirect objects. The principal purpose in using the passive in these sentences would be to focus attention on the person (**I.O.**), not on the "thing" (**D.O.**).

ANSWERS: **2.** Peggy has been awarded . . . by Indiana University.   **3.** Fred was paid . . . . [no "*by* phrase"]   **4.** Maria has been offered . . . by a local . . . .   **5.** You will be sent a bill . . . . [no "*by* phrase"]   **6.** The starving people will be given . . . . [no "*by* phrase"]

◇ **WORKBOOK:** Practice 9.

☐ **EXERCISE 7, p. 125.** *Changing active to passive.*

TECHNIQUE: *Oral (books closed).*

This should be a fast-paced exercise. You may want to add specific details to make the items relevant to your students' lives.

ANSWERS: **1.** I was invited . . . . [Note the change from question's "you" to answer's "I."] **2.** . . . book was written . . . .   **3.** (include the "*by* phrase")   **4.** Rice is grown . . . .   **5.** The letter is being typed by . . . .   **6.** The game is being televised.   **7.** Reading is taught in . . . . **8.** (. . .) has been offered a good job.   **9.** I was told to . . . .   **10.** That book was published in 1985.   **11.** (. . .) has been sent an . . . .   **12.** That hat was made in Mexico.   **13.** Dinner will be served at six.   **14.** . . . is going to be served.   **15.** The news will be announced . . . . **16.** The exam will be given next week.   **17.** The bill has been paid.   **18.** A mistake has been made.   **19.** The plants have been watered. [Note the plural verb.]   **20.** A test is being given (by the teacher) in . . . .   **21.** I am being asked (by the teacher) to . . . .

□ EXERCISE 8, p. 126.   *Using the passive in conversation.*

TECHNIQUE: *Oral (books closed); chain dialogue.*

You may not want to use every item in this exercise; just choose those that are apt to be most interesting to your students.

Each item will involve you and two students. Student A changes your cue to a passive sentence. Then you turn to Student B and ask a conversational question (from the second column) about the information in Student A's passive sentence. Student B then answers that question with a statement.

As the students speak, you should observe their pronunciation of *-ed* endings. Often students tend to omit the endings or to add unnecessary vowel sounds.

ANSWERS: **1.** A: My pen was stolen. B: It was stolen.   **2.** A: Spanish is spoken in many countries. B: Yes. It's spoken in many countries.   **3.** A: Soccer is played in many countries. B: (etc.)   **4.** That book was written by Mark Twain.   **5.** I went to a movie last night, but I was bored.   **6.** My letter was returned.   **7.** The bank was robbed.   **8.** The bank robber was caught (by the police).   **9.** The bank robber was sent to jail (by a judge). **10.** Each international student is required to have a visa.   **11.** This school was established in 1900.   **12.** There's a party tomorrow night, and I've been invited (to go). OR I've been invited (to go) to a party tomorrow night.   **13.** I was confused.   **14.** Gold was discovered in California in 1848.   **15.** A village was attacked by terrorists. OR He/She/The teacher read in the newspaper about a village that was attacked by terrorists.   **16.** Candles were used for light in the seventeenth century.   **17.** The hijacked plane was flown to another country.   **18.** When I had car trouble, I was helped by a passing motorist.   **19.** The coffee had already been made by the time I got up this morning.   **20.** The chair had already been sold by the time I returned to the store.

□ EXERCISE 9, p. 127.   *Using verb tenses with the passive.*

TECHNIQUE: *Controlled completion.*

This exercise can be done as written seatwork and then discussed, or it can be done orally. It works equally well with small groups and as a class exercise.

ANSWERS: **2.** is surrounded   **3.** is spelled/spelt   **4.** is going to/will be built   **5.** was/has been divided   **6.** is worn   **7.** was/had been caused   **8.** was ordered   **9.** was/had been killed   **10.** was reported   **11.** was surprised   **12.** was offered   **13.** were frightened **14.** was confused   **15.** is expected

□ EXERCISE 10, p. 128.   *Using active and passive appropriately.*

TECHNIQUE: *Fill-in-the-blanks.*

ANSWERS: **1.** is produced   **2.** will probably be won/is probably going to be won   **3.** saw . . . was interviewed   **4.** are controlled . . . are determined   **5.** blew . . . didn't want . . . (had) cost   **6.** is being treated   **7.** was caught . . . was being chased . . . jumped . . . kept [A "purse-snatcher" is a thief who steals a woman's purse.]   **8.** is exposed . . . affects ["Frostbite" is the formation of small ice crystals under the skin. In serious cases, it can result in severe damage to the skin.] [Point out that "affect" is a verb; "effect" is a noun.]   **9.** appeared . . . have been named and described [*Have been* is usually not repeated after *and*.] . . . are (being) discovered   **10.** has been poisoned ["First aid" is immediate medical treatment.] **11.** is supported ["It" refers to the school.]   **12.** was informed . . . was told ["Age discrimination" is a legal term similar to racial or sex discrimination. It refers to a situation in which someone is treated unfairly because of his/her age.]   **13.** were sent   **14.** was discovered . . . called . . . was translated . . . had been built . . . do not exist

◇ **WORKBOOK:** Practices 10, 11, 12, 13.

CHART 3-4: THE PASSIVE FORM OF MODALS

• ASSUMPTION: Students are familiar with the meanings of modal auxiliaries (Chapter 2).

• Students should note that there is no difference between singular and plural forms of the passive modals (modal + be . . . ; modal + have been . . .). Remind them that a modal is always followed immediately by the simple form of a verb. Similar expressions, such as *have to* and *be supposed to*, must agree in number with the subject.

• You might add examples relevant to your students' lives. Have them change passive sentences to active. Examples:

> *This room has to be cleaned.* → *Someone has to clean this room.*
> *Olga should be told about tomorrow's test.* → *Someone should tell Olga about . . . .*

☐ **EXERCISE 11, p. 130.** *Using active or passive with modals.*

TECHNIQUE: *Fill-in-the-blanks.*
Compare similar items so that students can see the differences in pairs of sentences where one is passive and the other is active. Encourage discussion of confusing items.

ANSWERS: **4.** must be kept **5.** must keep **6.** couldn't be opened **7.** couldn't open **8.** may be offered **9.** may offer **10.** may already have been offered **11.** may already have offered **12.** ought to be divided **13.** ought to have been divided **14.** have to be returned **15.** has to return **16.** had better be finished **17.** had better finish **18.** is supposed to be sent **19.** should have been sent **20.** must've been surprised

☐ **EXERCISE 12, p. 133.** *Using various modals with the passive.*

TECHNIQUE: *Fill-in-the-blanks.*
Encourage more than one answer to some of the items. Students usually enjoy experimenting with various combinations. In the following, the most likely answers are given first, and others are in parentheses.

ANSWERS:
  2. must be married [By custom, a wedding ring is worn on the next-to-last finger of the left hand.]
  3. have to/must be written (are to be written)
  4. must've been left
  5. should/ought to/has to be postponed (had better/must be postponed)
  6. shouldn't be given (must not be/can't be given)
  7. ought to/should be encouraged (must be encouraged)
  8. may/could/might/will be misunderstood
  9. can't be explained [A "UFO" is an Unidentified Flying Object, which some people believe comes from advanced civilizations on distant planets.]
  10. must've been embarrassed
  11. has to be pushed (must be pushed)
  12. should/ought to have been built
  13. must/should be saved (have to be/ought to be saved)
  14. must/has to be done (ought to be/should be done)
  15. ought to/should [advisability] /must/has to [necessity] /will [prediction] be elected (may/might/could [possibility] be elected) [Point out how the meaning significantly changes according to choice of modal.]

◇ **WORKBOOK:** Practices 14, 15, 16.

□ **EXERCISE 13, p. 134.**   *Creating sentences with the passive.*

TECHNIQUE: *Open completion.*
　　　Encourage students to create more than one sentence for each item. Because there are many items, you may wish to divide the students into groups, each with four or five items. Then each group can present their answers to the rest of the class, and discussion of alternatives may follow. This exercise may also be teacher-led with students' books closed.

ANSWERS:　[Depend on the students' creativity.]

CHART 3-5: STATIVE PASSIVE

• The stative passive is frequently used in both spoken and written English.

• You may want to demonstrate the relationship between "regular passive" and "stative passive" by using things in your classroom. Examples:

[Close a book.] *I just closed the book.*
　　　　The book was closed by me. [describes an action]
　　　　Now the book is closed. [describes an existing state]

[Have a student (Ali) break a piece of chalk.]

　　　　Ali broke the chalk.
　　　　The chalk was broken by Ali.
　　　　Now the chalk is broken.

□ **EXERCISE 14, p. 135.**   *Forming the stative passive.*

TECHNIQUE: *Fill-in-the-blanks.*

ANSWERS:　**2.** was closed [describes an existing state in the past.]　**3.** is made　**4.** is (not) shut　**5.** are bent . . . are folded　**6.** is finished [Contrast with the past active: "Class finished at 10 o'clock."]　**7.** are turned　**8.** is not crowded　**9.** is stuck ["To stick" = to be unable to move, as if glued.]　**10.** was stuck　**11.** is made . . . is swept . . . are washed　**12.** is set . . . are done . . . are lighted/lit　**13.** It's gone!　**14.** is torn　**15.** is hidden

□ **EXERCISE 15, p. 136.**   *Using the stative passive.*

TECHNIQUE: *Controlled completion.*

ANSWERS:　**2.** is . . . crowded　**3.** is scheduled　**4.** I'm exhausted.　**5.** I'm confused. **6.** are turned off　**7.** is insured　**8.** It's stuck.　**9.** are divorced　**10.** It's gone. **11.** are . . . qualified　**12.** am married　**13.** is spoiled/spoilt　**14.** is blocked　**15.** is located　**16.** was born　**17.** is . . . plugged in　**18.** are . . . done ["done" = "ready"]

◇ **WORKBOOK:** Practices 17 and 18.

□ **EXERCISE 16, p. 138.**   *Using prepositions with the stative passive.*

TECHNIQUE: *Fill-in-the-blanks.*
　　　You may wish to ask students to spell some of the verbs aloud to review the spelling rules in Chart 1-6, p. 9. [See Appendix 2 for a list of verbs with prepositions.]

ANSWERS:　**2.** is composed of　**3.** am accustomed to　**4.** is terrified of　**5.** is finished with　**6.** am opposed to　**7.** is covered with　**8.** am satisfied with　**9.** is married to **10.** is divorced from　**11.** am . . . acquainted with　**12.** am tired of　**13.** Are . . . related to

14. is dedicated to   **15.** is disappointed in/with   **16.** is scared of ["Scared of his own shadow" is an idiom describing someone who is very timid or shy.]   **17.** is committed to **18.** are devoted to   **19.** is dressed in   **20.** are done with

ADDITIONAL SUGGESTION: After the exercise is completed, ask the students to close their books. Quickly go through the whole exercise again orally by starting the sentence yourself, pausing for the students to supply a preposition, then finishing the sentence yourself. Use the same sentences in the book or make up your own. Example:

     TEACHER: *Ali is interested* . . . . [pause]
     STUDENTS: *in*
     TEACHER: *in ancient history (rock music/classical art,* etc.*).*

◇ **WORKBOOK:** Practices 19, 20, 21.

CHART 3-6: THE PASSIVE WITH *GET*	

• *Get* has a meaning similar to *become*; in other words, it signals a changing situation or an altered state. To discuss this meaning of *get*, you might ask students to make up their own sentences with *get* + adjective, using a few of the adjectives in the list in the chart's footnote.

☐ **EXERCISE 17, p. 139.**   *Using the passive with* get.

    TECHNIQUE: *Controlled completion.*
      Students can have fun if they read their answers rather dramatically, accompanied by gestures, as if performing in a theater.

    ANSWERS: **2.** I'm getting sleepy.   **3.** It's getting late.   **4.** got wet   **5.** It's getting hot **6.** get nervous   **7.** It's getting dark   **8.** got light   **9.** I'm getting full.   **10.** It's getting better.   **11.** Get busy. ["Shake a leg" = "get moving" = "step on it." All are idioms meaning to move or work faster, to hurry up.]   **12.** Get well [Point out that *well* is an adjective in this sentence and that a "get-well card" is sent only to someone who is ill.]

☐ **EXERCISE 18, p. 140.**   *Forming the passive with* get.

    TECHNIQUE: *Fill-in-the-blanks.*
      This is also a verb tense review exercise.

    ANSWERS: **2.** got hurt   **3.** got lost   **4.** get dressed   **5.** did . . . get married   **6.** get accustomed   **7.** am getting worried   **8.** get upset   **9.** got confused   **10.** get done **11.** got depressed   **12.** Did . . . get invited   **13.** got bored   **14.** get packed   **15.** get paid   **16.** got hired   **17.** got fired   **18.** didn't get finished   **19.** got disgusted   **20.** got engaged . . . got married . . . got divorced . . . got remarried

◇ **WORKBOOK:** Practices 22 and 23.

☐ **EXERCISE 19, p. 142.**   *Creating sentences with the passive and* get.

    TECHNIQUE: *Oral (books closed), open completion.*

    ANSWERS: [Depend on students' creativity.]

☐ **EXERCISE 20, p. 142.** *Review of verb tenses, active and passive.*

TECHNIQUE: *Fill-in-the-blanks.*

ANSWERS:
1. is usually/usually gets delivered
2. were working . . . occurred . . . was/got hurt
3. was not admitted (didn't get admitted) . . . had already begun
4. is spent [An amount of money is singular grammatically, even though the noun ends in -*s*. See Chart 5-15.]
5. was/got held up ["hold up" = delay] . . . took
6. had already been offered
7. will be used (is going to be used)
8. have been studying . . . is getting
9. is being organized
10. will never be forgotten (is never going to be forgotten)
11. arrive . . . will be met . . . will be wearing [at that moment] . . . is [an existing state] . . . has . . . will be standing
12. was . . . happened . . . flunked ["Flunk" (slang) = fail a test or a course in school.] . . . dropped . . . was walking . . . fell . . . was stolen ["You should have stayed in bed" is a common expression meaning "If you had not gotten out of bed this morning, you could have avoided all these problems."]

CHART 3-7: PARTICIPIAL ADJECTIVES

• The active meaning of the present participle (the -*ing* form of a verb) is also observed in the progressive. [See Chapter 1.]

• The passive meaning of the past participle (the -*ed* or irregular "third" form of a verb) is also observed in the passive, especially the stative passive.

☐ **EXERCISE 21, p. 144.** *Comparing adjectival present and past participles.*

TECHNIQUE: *Transformation, discussion of meaning.*
Encourage students to raise questions and discuss meanings during this exercise. You may want to explain that the present participle has an active ("giving" or "causing") meaning, but the past participle has a passive ("taking" or "receiving") meaning.

ANSWERS: **3.** exciting **4.** excited **5.** surprising **6.** surprised **7.** frightened **8.** frightening **9.** exhausting **10.** exhausted

☐ **EXERCISE 22, p. 144.** *Using participial adjectives.*

TECHNIQUE: *Oral (books closed), transformation.*

ANSWERS: **1.** amazing . . . amazed **2.** depressing . . . depressed **3.** tired . . . tiring **4.** boring . . . bored **5.** interested . . . interesting [etc.]

◇ **WORKBOOK:** Practice 24.

☐ **EXERCISE 23, p. 145.** *Using participial adjectives.*

TECHNIQUE: *Fill-in-the-blanks.*
Check on the spelling of the participles, especially "*y*" vs. "*i*" and doubling of consonants.

ANSWERS: **2.** satisfying **3.** terrifying **4.** terrified **5.** embarrassing **6.** broken

7. damaging   **8.** damaged   **9.** crowded. ["Elbowed" means to push people aside with one's elbow or arm.]   **10.** enduring [In this sense, "endure" means to last or continue for a long time.]   **11.** deserted   **12.** locked   **13.** lasting   **14.** injured   **15.** frozen

☐ **EXERCISE 24, p. 146.**   *Using participial adjectives.*

TECHNIQUE: *Fill-in-the-blanks.*

ANSWERS: **2.** annoying   **3.** given . . . following   **4.** challenging   **5.** expected
6. growing . . . balanced   **7.** sleeping [This saying means: "Don't change anything and cause problems."]   **8.** spoiled/spoilt [A child who is accustomed to receiving immediately everything he/she wants is said to be "spoiled," in other words unpleasant, like rotten food.]   **9.** leading
10. wasted   **11.** thrilling ["Hair-raising" means so frightening that it causes one's hair to stand up on one's neck or head.]   **12.** flying   **13.** abandoned [A "tow truck" is a service vehicle that pulls broken-down cars.]   **14.** thinking   **15.** required   **16.** bustling ["bustling" = busy, somewhat noisy, crowded]

◇ **WORKBOOK:** Practices 25 and 26.

☐ **EXERCISE 25, p. 147.**   *Correct usage of the passive, tenses, spelling, etc.*

TECHNIQUE: *Error analysis.*

ANSWERS: **1.** interest**ed**   **2.** peopl**e** [no *-s*] . . . have you [no *been*] invited   **3.** everything **was quiet** . . . walk**ed** . . . go**t** undress**ed** . . . **went**   **4.** had already [no *been*] eaten   **5.** confus**ed**
6. frighten**ed**   **7.** we **were** very . . . [possibly *those*—in the past, therefore distant; *these* is also acceptable] . . . we ran . . . scar**ed** . . . **see**   **8.** axe **fell** . . . began . . . **did** not

◇ **WORKBOOK:** Practices 27, 28, 29.

☐ **EXERCISE 26, p. 148.**   *Using tenses, active, passive, etc., in writing.*

TECHNIQUE: *Written homework.*
    Tell the class how long you expect their compositions to be. Discuss possible methods of organization: for example, an introductory paragraph followed by several paragraphs containing a chronological summary of the person's life, leading to a conclusion about that person's life.
    Sometimes students tend to overuse the passive for a while after they have been concentrating on it in class. Remind them that most sentences are active. Most of the sentences in this exercise will be active, but the passive will also occur (*was born, was married, is interested in, has always been committed to*, etc.).

◇ **WORKBOOK:** Have students take Practice Test A and/or B.

☐ **EXERCISE 27, p. 148.**   *Phrasal verbs.*

TECHNIQUE: *Seatwork, fill-in-the-blanks, teacher-led oral.*
    [See Appendix 2 for a list of common two-word and three-word verbs.]

ANSWERS: **1.** in   **2.** on . . . off   **3.** back   **4.** in/by [*Over* is also possible.]   **5.** out
6. out   **7.** up   **8.** up . . . away   **9.** out [Note: One "fills *out*" a large item such as an application form, but "fills *in*" a small space such as a blank in an exercise. Also: "fill *up*" (British) = "fill *in*" (American).] . . . back   **10.** up ["catch up with him" (American) = "catch him up" (British)]   **11.** on   **12.** out

Chapter 4: GERUNDS AND INFINITIVES

ORDER OF CHAPTER	CHARTS	EXERCISES	WORKBOOK
Form of gerunds	4-1		
Gerunds as the objects of prepositions	4-2	Ex. 1 → 4	Pr. 1 → 2
Verbs followed by gerunds	4-3 → 4-4	Ex. 5 → 7	Pr. 3
Cumulative review and practice		Ex. 8	
Verbs followed by infinitives	4-5	Ex. 9 → 11	Pr. 4 → 6
Verbs followed by infinitives or gerunds	4-6	Ex. 12	Pr. 7
Cumulative review and practice		Ex. 13 → 15	Pr. 8
Reference lists of verbs	4-7 → 4-8	Ex. 16 → 17	Pr. 9 → 13
Gerunds as subjects	4-9	Ex. 18	Pr. 14
It + infinitive	4-9	Ex. 19 → 21	Pr. 15
Infinitive of purpose	4-10	Ex. 22 → 23	Pr. 16
Infinitives with adjectives, *too, enough*	4-11 → 4-12	Ex. 24 → 27	Pr. 17 → 18
Passive gerunds and infinitives	4-13 → 4-14	Ex. 28 → 30	Pr. 19 → 22
Gerunds with possessive modifiers	4-15	Ex. 31	Pr. 23
Cumulative review and practice		Ex. 32	Pr. 24 → 25
Special verbs and expressions	4-16 → 4-19	Ex. 33 → 37	Pr. 26 → 30
Cumulative review and practice		Ex. 38 → 41	Pr. 31 → 35 Pr. Tests A & B

General Notes on Chapter 4

• OBJECTIVE: Gerunds and infinitives are common features of both spoken and written English (as the following underlines demonstrate). A person who tries to speak English without using gerunds and infinitives will produce very unnatural-sounding sentences. Learning to understand and use these structures fluently is important for students.

- APPROACH: The chapter begins with gerunds and their functions, then introduces infinitives, then special groups of verbs followed by either a gerund or an infinitive. Next, other uses of gerunds and infinitives are presented, and then uses of the simple form are introduced. Throughout, the emphasis is on becoming comfortable with these structures through practice, not memorization. The cumulative exercises include review of various verb tenses and the passive, which were introduced in earlier chapters.

- TERMINOLOGY: Like many traditional terms in grammar, "gerund" and "infinitive" were borrowed from analyses of the Latin language; they do not fit the description of the English language equally as well. In this text, the combination "*to* + simple form of a verb" is called an **infinitive** (*to be, to fly*). The **"simple" form of a verb** is the base form with no indication of tense or number (*be, fly*). A **gerund** is a "verb + *ing*" that functions like a noun (*being, flying*).

CHART 4-1: GERUNDS: INTRODUCTION

- Students should learn that "gerund" is the name of a <u>form</u> based on a verb. A gerund may have the <u>function</u> of subject or object in a sentence.

- In Chapter 1, students learned that some verbs (such as *know, need, want*) usually have no progressive form, and they may hesitate to use the *-ing* form of these verbs. Point out that these verbs can be used as gerunds:
      INCORRECT: *I am knowing John.* [progressive form is not appropriate]
      CORRECT: *<u>Knowing John</u> is a pleasure.* [gerund as subject]
      CORRECT: *I insist on <u>knowing the truth</u>.* [gerund as object of a preposition]

- Because a gerund is based on a verb form, it can have an object and be modified by adverbial phrases.
      I <u>play games</u>. = vb + obj → *<u>Playing games</u> is fun.* = gerund + obj
      We <u>play in the park</u>. = vb + prep. phr. → *<u>Playing in the park</u> is fun.* = gerund + prep. phr.
      → *<u>Playing games in the park</u> is fun.* = gerund + obj + prep. phr

- You may wish to introduce the term "gerund phrase." A gerund with its associated object or modifier is called a "gerund phrase." In the above examples, *playing games, playing in the park,* and *playing games in the park* are gerund phrases.

CHART 4-2: USING GERUNDS AS THE OBJECTS OF PREPOSITIONS

- A gerund can immediately follow a preposition, but an infinitive cannot.

- The exception that proves the rule: in one idiom, a preposition is followed by an infinitive, not by a gerund: *be about,* meaning "ready for immediate action." For example: *I am <u>about to open</u> my book.*

☐ **EXERCISE 1, p. 151.*** *Gerunds after prepositions.*

After students work out a few of the answers, you might divide the class in half and do this exercise orally and rather quickly. As a variation, you read aloud from the book, pause for one group to say the preposition, signal the other group to say the gerund, then finish the sentence yourself. For example:

---

*The types of exercises in this chapter are similar to those in the preceding three chapters. See the INTRODUCTION, pp. ix–xvii, for suggestions about techniques for using exercises.

TEACHER: *Alice isn't interested . . . .*[pause]
GROUP A: *in*
GROUP B: *looking*
TEACHER: *in looking for a new job.*

Group B's answer will always be a gerund, thus underscoring the main point of Chart 4-2.

Appendix 2 contains a list of prepositional combinations with verbs and adjectives. The students can refer to it if they wish.

ANSWERS: **2.** about leaving   **3.** of doing   **4.** for being   **5.** to having [possible in British English: *to have*]   **6.** from completing   **7.** about having   **8.** of studying   **9.** for helping   **10.** (up)on knowing   **11.** by drawing [*By* + gerund = **how** something is done; see Exercise 4.]   **12.** of living   **13.** for not going   **14.** in searching   **15.** for making   **16.** for not wanting   **17.** for washing and drying [Point out parallel structure.]   **18.** to going   **19.** from speaking   **20.** to going   **21.** of clarifying   **22.** of stealing   **23.** of taking . . . (of) keeping [parallel structure]   **24.** to wearing   **25.** to eating . . . (to) sleeping [parallel structure]

☐ **EXERCISE 2, p. 152.**   *Using gerunds after prepositions.*

You may wish to point out that short answers ("Yes, she did.") are more natural in response to conversational questions. However, in this exercise the students should respond with complete sentences in order to practice using gerunds.

ANSWERS:
1. Yes, I had a good excuse for being late . . ./No, I didn't have . . . .
2. Yes, I'm (really) looking forward to visiting them./No, I'm not looking . . . .
3. Yes, I thanked him/her for picking it up./No, I didn't thank . . . .
4. No, I'm not accustomed to living . . ./Yes, I'm accustomed to living . . . .
5. Yes, I'm excited about going . . ./No, I'm not excited about going . . . .
6. Yes, I apologized . . . ./No, I didn't apologize for interrupting her . . . .
7. Yes, all of them participated in doing . . ./No, some of them did not participate in doing the pantomimes.
8. No, I don't know . . ./Yes, I know who is responsible for breaking . . . .
9. No, I'm not used to having . . ./Yes, I'm used to having my biggest meal . . . .
10. The hot/cold weather prevents me from (. . .)ing . . . .
11. No, s/he doesn't complain . . ./Yes, s/he complains about having to do a lot of homework.
12. No, I don't blame him/her for staying home in bed. [A negative answer is expected.]
13. S/He [past tense verb] instead of studying.
14. In addition to studying grammar last night, I [past tense verb].

☐ **EXERCISE 3, p. 153.**   *Using gerund phrases after prepositions.*

This can be done as individual homework or small group seatwork. Then some sentences can be written on the chalkboard and discussed. Alternatively, students can simply call out their completions.

ANSWERS: **2.** . . . for lending me (her dictionary).   **3.** . . . about going to . . . .   **4.** . . . to living (in . . .)   **5.** . . . about having (a headache).   **6.** . . . for not wanting (another roommate).   **7.** . . . for being (late).   **8.** . . . about missing (my bus).   **9.** . . . in finding out about . . . .   **10.** about going . . . .   **11.** . . . for being . . . .   **12.** . . . to driving (fast).   **13.** . . . from going . . . .   **14.** . . . for taking care of . . . ?

◇ **WORKBOOK:** Practices 1 and 2.

□ **EXERCISE 4, p. 154.** *Using* by + *a gerund.*

You can read the beginning of a sentence and have one or two students finish it by calling out their completions. Discuss any problems.

POSSIBLE ANSWERS: [Depend on students' ideas.]

CHART 4-3: COMMON VERBS FOLLOWED BY GERUNDS

• This chart and the next exercises present just a few of the verbs that are followed by gerunds. Students may want to memorize the list, but a more effective way to learn them is to practice them both orally and in writing.

□ **EXERCISE 5, p. 155.** *Using gerunds after certain verbs.*

Encourage the students to use various tenses and to include interesting information in their sentences.

ANSWERS: [Depend on students' creativity.]

□ **EXERCISE 6, p. 155.** *Using gerunds.*

POSSIBLE ANSWERS: **2.** Opening/closing/shutting **3.** raining/snowing **4.** running/going **5.** going for/taking **6.** studying/working **7.** having/giving/hosting, etc. **8.** laughing/giggling **9.** crashing into/colliding with/hitting/running into **10.** going/travel(l)ing **11.** doing/starting **12.** making **13.** going/flying **14.** taking/riding **15.** being

---

CHART 4-4: *GO* + **GERUND**

• Some grammarians disagree about the nature of these *-ing* words: are they gerunds or participles? For your students, terminology is much less important than idiomatic use. We will call these structures gerunds.

• Definitions of some vocabulary items in the chart:

birdwatching = a hobby for people who enjoy identifying birds in natural habitats
bowling = an indoor sport in which a heavy ball is rolled toward 9 or 10 wooden pins to knock them down
camping = living in a tent or trailer for fun; "getting back to nature"
canoeing = floating on a river or lake in a small, simple boat called a canoe (pronounced /kə-**nu**/)
hiking = athletic walking in the mountains or countryside (possibly while carrying equipment in a pack on one's back = *to go backpacking*)
jogging = running somewhat slowly for exercise
sailing = floating on a lake or sea in a boat that has a sail or perhaps a motor for power
sightseeing = touring; traveling to see famous or beautiful places
sledding = in winter, going down a snowy hill using a sled, which is a wooden seat on metal bars that can slide quickly over the snow
tobogganing = similar to sledding; a toboggan is a long, flat wooden structure for several people to sit on while going down a snowy hill
window shopping = looking into shop windows, but perhaps not intending to buy anything

• Depending upon their cultural attitudes, students may enjoy learning the expression *go skinny dipping* (to go swimming without a bathing suit).

□ **EXERCISE 7, p. 156.** *Verbs & gerunds.*

This can be used for pair or group work as an alternative to teacher-led oral. All of the sentences require the use of gerunds.

ANSWERS: [Depend on students' ideas.] Note that items 8, 10, 12, 14, and 18 have two gerunds together; e.g., **8.** . . . talk(ed) about *going swimming* . . . .

◇ **WORKBOOK:** Practice 3.

CHART 4-5: COMMON VERBS FOLLOWED BY INFINITIVES

• The passive examples (f) and (g) assume that students are familiar with the basic forms in Chapter 3. If they aren't, you may need to explain them, because the passive is used in Exercises 8 through 11.

• The alternative structures in the notes below this chart are important for the following exercise. You should call the students' attention to these sentences.

◇ **WORKBOOK:** Practice 4.

□ **EXERCISE 8, p. 157.** *Verbs followed by infinitives or gerunds.*

POSSIBLE ANSWERS: **3.** to find/look for/get **4.** to do/hand in **5.** playing/watching **6.** to lend/loan **7.** to come **8.** to finish ["ASAP" is spoken as individual letters, not as a word. It is not often used outside an office context.] **9.** to get/buy **10.** to be . . . talking **11.** getting . . . to wait **12.** to use **13.** to write **14.** not to touch **15.** being/living, etc. **16.** to be **17.** (not) to know **18.** to write **19.** to own/keep/have **20.** to take **21.** to mail/open/hold, etc. **22.** to mail/open **23.** to find **24.** to find **25.** finding **26.** finding **27.** to take **28.** taking

□ **EXERCISE 9, p. 159.** *Verbs + infinitives to report speech.*

The answers are in the form of reported (or indirect) speech. The cues are in quoted (or direct) speech. Chapter 7 contains charts 7-6 and 7-7 on quoted and reported speech, but students probably don't need that lesson in order to complete this exercise. Students can understand that verb + infinitive is a way of reporting what someone has said. You may wish to point out the equivalency between modals/imperatives in quoted speech and verb + infinitive in reported speech. Or you may wish not to discuss the concept of quoted vs. reported speech at all.

Show the students how item 1 was produced. Give them time to write their answers. Then review all their answers orally, with each student reading one answer aloud. Discussion can follow each item that causes difficulty.

ANSWERS: **2.** The secretary asked me to give this note to Sue./I was asked to give this note to Sue. **3.** My advisor advised me to take Biology 109. [This rather awkward sentence includes both "advisor" and "advised."]/I was advised to take Biology 109. [This sentence avoids the awkwardness.] **4.** When . . . , the judge ordered me to pay . . . /. . . , I was ordered to pay . . . . **5.** During . . . , the teacher warned Greg to keep his eyes on his own paper./. . . Greg was warned to keep his . . . . **6.** During . . . , the teacher warned Greg not to look at his neighbor's paper./. . . , Greg was warned not to look . . . . **7.** At . . . , the head of the department reminded the faculty to turn in their . . . /. . . , the faculty were (OR was) reminded to turn in their . . . . **8.** Mr. Lee told the children to be quiet./The children were told to be quiet. **9.** The hijacker forced the pilot to land the plane./The pilot was forced to . . . . [A hijacker is someone who takes control of a plane, train, bus, etc. by force.] **10.** When . . . , my parents allowed me to stay up late . . . / . . . , I was allowed to stay up late . . . . **11.** The teacher encouraged the students to speak slowly and clearly./The students were encouraged to speak slowly and clearly. **12.** The teacher always expects the students to come to class on time./The students are always expected to come . . .

☐ **EXERCISE 10, p. 161.** *Using verbs followed by infinitives.*

You may want to allow students to work in small groups. Then, an individual can read the cue aloud rather dramatically, and two other students can read the reported forms. No "*by* -phrase" should be included in the answers.

ANSWERS:
   2. The general ordered the soldiers to surround. . ./The soldiers were ordered to surround . . . .
   3. Nancy asked me to open the window./I was asked to . . . .
   4. Bob reminded me to take my book . . ./I was reminded to . . . .
   5. Paul encouraged/advised me to take singing lessons./I was advised to take . . . .
   6. Mrs. Anderson warned the children not to play with matches./The children were warned not to . . . .
   7. The Dean of Admissions permitted me to register for school late./I was permitted to register . . . .
   8. The law requires every driver to have a . . ./Every driver is required to have a . . . .
   9. My friend advised me to get . . ./I was advised to get . . . .
   10. The robber forced me to give him all of my money./I was forced to give (the robber) all of my money (to the robber). [either position]
   11. Before . . . , the teacher advised/told/warned/reminded the students to work quickly. [The choice of verb gives information about *how* the teacher spoke to the students.]/Before . . . , the students were . . . to work quickly.
   12. My boss asked/advised/ordered/reminded/told me to come . . ./I was . . . to come . . . . [Again, the verb contains important information about *how* the boss spoke.]

◇ **WORKBOOK:** Practices 5 and 6.

☐ **EXERCISE 11, p. 161.** *Verbs followed by infinitives, active/passive.*

This exercise follows the same pattern as Exercises 9 and 10. Students should now be able to use their own ideas to create appropriate sentences.

ANSWERS: [Depend on students' ideas.]

CHART 4-6: COMMON VERBS FOLLOWED BY EITHER INFINITIVES OR GERUNDS

• The complex history of the English language—elements from German, French, Norse, etc.—has produced the parallel forms in Group A. Learners should be confident that using the infinitive or gerund with these verbs causes no real change in meaning.

• Native speakers of English do not always agree on the use of the forms in Group A. Some differences exist among speakers in various geographical regions.

• The differences with Group B verbs are great, and students need practice in order to understand and use them appropriately. Using an infinitive instead of a gerund with one of these verbs causes a significant change in meaning.

☐ **EXERCISES 12 & 13, pp. 163–165.** *Choosing between gerunds and infinitives.*

The answers to these two exercises will probably raise many questions that need to be discussed briefly. Therefore, it is best to do the two orally with the whole class, although you might have students work in small groups on Exercise 13.

EX. 12 ANSWERS: **2.** to leave/leaving **3.** to lecture/lecturing **4.** to swim/swimming **5.** to see/seeing [*Living* is a present participle (adjective) that modifies the gerund (noun) *being*; a living being is a human or an animal.] **6.** to move/moving . . . to race/racing . . . to move . . . to race [Choose the infinitive after a progressive verb.] **7.** driving . . . taking **8.** to drive . . . (to) take [Some people might also use gerunds.] **9.** to turn **10.** being **11.** to give **12.** playing **13.** doing **14.** to do **15.** to do **16.** carrying [It is traditional for a husband to carry his new wife through the doorway (over the threshold) of their first home.] **17.** watching **18.** to do **19.** to inform **20.** not listening **21.** to explain **22.** holding . . . feeding . . . burping [to burp = (to cause) to belch or to expel air from the stomach through the mouth] . . . changing.

EX. 13 ANSWERS: **2.** cleaning **3.** to take **4.** to leave **5.** to talk/talking **6.** waiting . . . doing **7.** to stay . . . paint [*To* is usually not repeated after *and*.] **8.** quitting . . . opening **9.** to take **10.** looking . . . to answer **11.** postponing **12.** watching . . . listening **13.** to read/reading **14.** to go camping ["To go to camp" includes the <u>noun</u> *camp* after the preposition *to*—not an infinitive.] **15.** singing **16.** to take . . . to pay **17.** to stand **18.** not to wait

◇ **WORKBOOK:** Practice 7.

☐ **EXERCISE 14, p. 166.** *Using infinitives and gerunds after verbs.*

This is a good opportunity to review verb tenses, singular-plural agreement, and modals as well as infinitives and gerunds. You may want to follow the oral exercise with an assignment for the students to write 10 or 15 of their best sentences for homework. Or you could turn the exercise into a quiz, with the students writing sentences from your spoken cues.

ANSWERS: [Depend on students' creativity.]

☐ **EXERCISE 15, p. 166.** *Using infinitives and gerunds after verbs.*

This is a review of Chapter 4 to this point.

ANSWERS: **1.** talking **2.** to play . . . not to make **3.** to look after **4.** paying **5.** to chase/chasing **6.** going . . . to go **7.** going skiing **8.** not to smoke **9.** not to know/not knowing **10.** whistling . . . to concentrate **11.** to quit . . . (to) look for **12.** to turn off [*Turning off* would give a quite different meaning and would be unlikely in this situation; possibly one might say, "Think carefully. Do you remember turning off the stove? We don't want our house to burn down!" Also: *stove = cooker* in British English.] **13.** to renew **14.** not to wait **15.** not to play **16.** to call **17.** to throw away . . . (to) buy [The second *to* is usually omitted in parallel structure.] **18.** dropping out of . . . hitchhiking . . . trying to find **19.** to tell . . . to call . . . going swimming **20.** to ask . . . to tell . . . to remember to bring

◇ **WORKBOOK:** Practice 8.

CHARTS 4-7 and 4-8: REFERENCE LISTS OF VERBS FOLLOWED BY GERUNDS OR INFINITIVES

• These lists are for students to refer to, not to memorize. The following exercises and the workbook provide a lot of practice, but learners don't have to learn the lists by heart.

• Ask for and answer any questions about vocabulary.

• You could create an oral (books closed) exercise using these charts. Select some of the sentences at random and ask students to put the verbs in their proper gerund or infinitive forms. For example:

TEACHER (choosing #7 from Section A in Chart 4-8): "I don't care" [pause] "see that show."
STUDENT: "I don't care to see that show."
TEACHER: (Perhaps repeat the correct answer. Then choose another item, such as #5 from Chart 4-7): "He avoided" [pause] "answer my question."
STUDENT: "He avoided answering my/your question."
etc.

☐ **EXERCISE 16, p. 170.** *Choosing between gerunds and infinitives.*

This is a mechanical exercise so that students can focus on choosing the gerund or the infinitive after certain verbs. The whole class can answer together. As suggested in the book, you could then repeat the exercise, with individual students using their own words to complete each sentence.

ANSWERS:

1. to do it	**11.** to do it	**21.** to do it	**31.** doing it
2. doing it	**12.** to do it	**22.** doing it?	**32.** to do it
3. to do it	**13.** to do it	**23.** doing it?	**33.** to do it
4. to do it	**14.** doing it	**24.** to do it	**34.** to do it
5. to do it	**15.** to do it	**25.** doing it	**35.** doing it
6. doing it	**16.** to do it	**26.** doing it	**36.** to do it
7. doing it	**17.** to do it	**27.** to do it	**37.** to do it
8. to do it	**18.** to do it	**28.** doing it	**38.** doing it
9. doing it	**19.** doing it	**29.** to do it?	**39.** doing it
10. doing it	**20.** to do it	**30.** doing it	**40.** doing it

☐ **EXERCISE 17, p. 170.** *Using gerunds and infinitives.*

If they did Exercise 16 well, students should be able to complete most of these sentences without looking at the reference charts. However, they may have trouble remembering some items, so you might allow them to look at the charts or to discuss those problems briefly with each other.

ANSWERS:

1. to race	**7.** to know	**13.** worrying	**19.** to have
2. to bring	**8.** being	**14.** to play	**20.** being
3. pronouncing	**9.** telling	**15.** telling	**21.** hearing
4. to eat	**10.** to be	**16.** taking	**22.** promising to visit
5. to hang up	**11.** to do	**17.** to buy	**23.** hoping . . . praying
6. to pull	**12.** to return . . . (to) finish	**18.** to change	**24.** to persuade . . . to stay . . . (to) finish

◇ **WORKBOOK:** Practices 9, 10, 11, 12, 13.

CHART 4-9: USING GERUNDS AS SUBJECTS: USING *IT* + INFINITIVE

• You may need to point out that a gerund subject is singular and requires a singular form of the verb: *Playing games is fun.*

• The emphasis in Chart 4-9 and Exercises 18 to 21 is on the *it* + *infinitive* structure, a frequent pattern in both speech and writing.

• Of course, *it* + *gerund* is also possible, and some students may produce some examples. Also, an infinitive can be the subject of a sentence. Commend students if they use these correctly, but return their attention to the more common *it* + *infinitive* and *gerund as subject* patterns in this lesson.

☐ **EXERCISE 18, p. 172.** *Gerunds as subjects.*

After giving the example, ask students to complete the same sentence with other gerund phrases. Ask for several different responses for each item so that students have a chance to think of meaningful sentences in this pattern. Encourage them to use a whole phrase (e.g., "climbing to the top of a mountain"), not just the gerund.

ANSWERS: [Depend on students' creativity.]

☐ **EXERCISE 19, p. 172.** *Gerund vs. it + infinitive.*

Students can work in pairs, or one student in class can read the item and another respond. This is a mechanical exercise, allowing students to focus on the forms. They should understand that both forms of a sentence have the same meaning.

ANSWERS: **3.** It is important to vote . . . . **4.** Meeting the king and queen was exciting. **5.** It would be interesting to hear . . . . **6.** Seeing Joan awake . . . is unusual. **7.** If you know how, floating in water for a long time is easy. **8.** It takes time and patience to master . . . . **9.** It will take us ten hours to drive to Atlanta. **10.** Diving into the sea from a high cliff takes courage.

☐ **EXERCISE 20, p. 173.** *Using gerunds and infinitives.*

Students must listen carefully to each other in this exercise. Student A's answer is used by Student B. As with Exercise 18, you could ask for several different responses to each item for additional practice.

ANSWERS: [Depend on students' creativity.]

☐ **EXERCISE 21, p. 173.** *Using for (someone) + infinitive.*

This exercise has two purposes. One is to teach the correct **location** of the "*for (someone)*" phrase between the adjective and the infinitive. (For example, it is incorrect in English to say *It is important to go for me./It for me is important to go./It is for me important to go.*)
The other purpose is to demonstrate the **meaning** and **use** of the "*for (someone)*" phrase. It limits the meaning of a general statement. For example, item 3 ("It's easy to speak Spanish.") is not true for most people, so it's necessary to limit that statement to some person or group ("It's easy for Venezuelans to speak Spanish.").

POSSIBLE ANSWERS: **3.** It's easy for Carlos to speak Spanish. **4.** It's important for us to learn English so that we can read scientific books. **5.** It's unusual for Jerry to be late for dinner because he's always hungry.   **6.** It's essential for you to get a visa if you plan to visit the Soviet Union on your trip next summer. Etc.

◇ **WORKBOOK:** Practices 14 and 15.

CHART 4-10: INFINITIVE OF PURPOSE: *IN ORDER TO*

• Additional examples for the footnote:

(general) *An encyclopedia is used for locating facts and information.*
(specific) *I used the encyclopedia to locate facts about India.*

(general) *Knives are used for cutting or slicing.*
(specific) *My brother used a knife to cut his birthday cake.*

☐ **EXERCISE 22, p. 174.**   *Typical errors with infinitives of purpose.*

Allow students some time to find errors in the sentences, then lead the class in a discussion of their corrections.

ANSWERS: **1.** Helen borrowed my dictionary *(in order) to* look up . . . .   **2.** I went to the library *(in order) to* study last night.   **3.** The teacher opened the window *(in order) to* get some fresh air in the room.   **4.** I came to this school *(in order) to* learn English.   **5.** I need to get a part-time job *(in order) to* earn . . . .

☐ **EXERCISE 23, p. 174.**   *Using infinitives and prepositions of purpose.*

This exercise contrasts the infinitive of purpose (*in order to*) with a prepositional phrase of purpose (*for* + noun). Encourage students to give more than one completion for each item.

POSSIBLE ANSWERS: **3.** . . . to buy some soap.   **4.** . . . for some soap.   **5.** . . . to have my blood pressure checked.   **6.** . . . for a checkup.   **7.** . . . to keep in shape.   **8.** . . . for health and fitness.   **9.** . . . to get some gas(oline)/petrol.   **10.** . . . for gas(oline)/petrol.

ADDITIONAL PRACTICE: Here is an Oral (books closed) exercise from the first edition of the textbook. It enables you to give additional communicative practice using the students' names and couching the cue in familiar situations. For example:
　　CUE:　(. . .) went to the library. He/She wanted to study.
　　TEACHER:　*Ali is a good student. He studies every night. Last night he went to the library. He wanted to study grammar. Why did Ali go to the library?* (Ask one student or all.)
　　STUDENT(S):　*He went to the library (in order) to study grammar.*
　1. (. . .) picked up the phone. She wanted to call her husband./He wanted to call his wife.
　　TEACHER:　*Yesterday Tania was at home. Dinner was ready, but her husband still wasn't home. He was at his office. She decided to call him. Why did Tania pick up the phone?* [**Answer:** . . . to call her husband and ask why he wasn't home.]
　2. Before class, (. . .) walked to the front of the room. He/She wanted to ask me a question.
　3. (. . .) took out his/her dictionary. He/She wanted to look up a word.
　4. (. . .) wants to improve his/her English. He/She reads a lot of books and magazines.
　5. (. . .) wanted to pay his/her bill at the restaurant. He/She took out his/her wallet.
　6. (. . .) turned off the lights. He/She wanted to save energy.
　7. (. . .) turned on the stove/cooker. He/She wanted to heat some water for tea.

◇ **WORKBOOK:** Practice 16.

CHART 4-11: ADJECTIVES FOLLOWED BY INFINITIVES

• This list is not complete; however, many of the most frequently used adjectives are included here.

• Many of these adjectives can be followed by other structures. For example:
   I was *happy about going* to the circus. (preposition + gerund)
   I was *happy watching* the clouds float by. (present participle)
It is not necessary to mention these structures to the learners at this point. Their focus should remain on *adjective + infinitive*.

☐ **EXERCISE 24, p. 175.** *Adjectives followed by infinitives.*

EXPECTED ANSWERS: **3.** to be   **4.** to die/to surrender/to fight   **5.** to go   **6.** to stay . . . read [*To* is usually not repeated after *and*.]   **7.** to help   **8.** to study/to learn   **9.** to slip/to fall   **10.** to walk   **11.** to walk/to drive/to go/to stay/to be   **12.** to be   **13.** to see   **14.** to hear/to learn/to read

☐ **EXERCISE 25, p. 176.** *Using infinitives after adjectives.*

This exercise can be done as a dialogue between you and the students or as student-student pair work. If the contexts seem unreal or inappropriate for your situation, you may want to substitute other items. No exercise in this book can be perfect for every circumstance, so you should consider changing some items to suit your needs.

ANSWERS: [Depend on students' ideas.]

◇ **WORKBOOK:** Practice 17.

CHART 4-12: USING INFINITIVES WITH *TOO* AND *ENOUGH*

• Learners of English often fail to understand that the word *too* before an adjective has a negative meaning.

• The word order with *enough* is important to practice: it comes <u>after</u> an adjective or adverb but usually <u>before</u> a noun. Note the difference in structure and meaning:

   (a) We don't have ***enough* big envelopes.** = We have an insufficient number; *enough* modifies the noun *envelopes*.
   (b) We don't have **big *enough* envelopes.** = Our envelopes are too small; *enough* modifies the adjective *big*.

☐ **EXERCISE 26, p. 177.** *Using too with infinitives.*

Students must understand what a "negative result" is. In item 1, for example, the speaker obviously wants to buy a ring. But, because the ring is *too* expensive, the result is negative: he/she is <u>not able</u> to buy the ring.

POSSIBLE ANSWERS: **3.** I can't get to class on time. It's too late for me to . . . .   **4.** We can't go swimming. It's too cold for us to . . . .   **5.** I don't want to study it. It's too . . . for me . . . .   **6.** I can't watch TV now. I'm too busy to . . . .   **7.** He shouldn't play football. He's too young to . . . .   **8.** They can't climb the cliff. It's too steep for them to . . . .   **10.** I can go to the meeting. I'm not too tired to . . . .   **11.** I can lift/carry it . . . .   **12.** I can watch TV now . . . .

◇ **WORKBOOK:** Practice 18.

☐ **EXERCISE 27, p. 178.** *Using* enough *and* too *with infinitives.*

> Because the students' books are closed, you may need to repeat a cue or add some brief contextual information to help them understand the cue. This exercise intends to touch upon typical student misunderstandings in the use of *too* instead of *very* (e.g., INCORRECT: *My country is too beautiful.*).
>
> *POSSIBLE ANSWERS:*
> 1. A child is too young to read a long novel, but an adult is old enough to appreciate good literature. [Have the students come up with various ideas, then compare "too young" with "very young" in item #2.]
> 2. She's very young. [Also: She's old enough/not too young to begin walking and talking.]
> 3. very [Note: In the negative, *too* and *very* can express the same idea: "It wasn't too good/It wasn't very good." = "I didn't like it much." But here the cue says it _was_ a good dinner.]
> 4. very ["It's *too* difficult" = "It's impossible to learn," which is not true. Perhaps give your students a pep talk and praise their progress.]
> 5. very [Ask your students if something can be "too clean."]
> 6. very OR too [depending on student's idea, with *too* implying negative result]
> 7. [demonstrate *enough* and *too*]
> 8. very
> 9. very [The highest mountain in the world is Mt. Everest: 5.5 miles, 8.9 kilometers above sea level; approximately 29,000 feet or 8,800 meters.]
> 10. [Discuss placement of *enough*: when it follows a noun, it may seem somewhat formal or literary. In everyday English, it usually comes in front of a noun.]

CHART 4-13: PAST AND PASSIVE FORMS OF INFINITIVES AND GERUNDS

• Chapter 3 presents the passive. You may wish to review the notions of "passive verb" and "*by*-phrase" with your students.

• Students may want to consult the reference lists of verbs followed by infinitives or gerunds, pp. 168–169.

• The following chart might be helpful for your students when you explain that an infinitive or gerund can be either simple or past, and that these forms can be either passive or active.

		SIMPLE	PAST
ACTIVE	inf:	to see	to have seen
	ger:	seeing	having seen
PASSIVE	inf:	to be seen	to have been seen
	ger:	being seen	having been seen

◇ **WORKBOOK:** Practices 19 and 20.

☐ **EXERCISE 28, p. 179.** *Passive & past forms of infinitives & gerunds.*

> This exercise requires students to think about tenses, verbs that require infinitives or gerunds, and relationships in time. Allow plenty of time for them to prepare their answer to an item, then discuss any misunderstanding.

As the footnote on page 179 explains, sometimes a simple gerund can be used with a past tense main verb even though the gerund's action occurred earlier in time. This shows that the English language is changing—not everyone always uses these forms in the same way. But both forms are still in common use, so students need to learn their normal functions.

ANSWERS: **4.** being hit ["barely" = almost unable] **5.** to be told [by us] **6.** having written **7.** having been asked [Note: Something that has a base (a building, a candle) is usually said to "burn down." Other things "burn up."] **8.** to have been given **9.** being told **10.** to be loved . . . needed [*To be* is usually not repeated in the parallel structure.] **11.** watching **12.** not having written [*sooner* = earlier, before now]

☐ **EXERCISE 29, p. 180.** *Passive & past forms of infinitives & gerunds.*

ANSWERS: **1.** being photographed **2.** to have escaped **3.** to have had **4.** having gone **5.** meeting/having met **6.** to be sent **7.** to be told **8.** to have recovered . . . to be **9.** having had **10.** having **11.** not having been told . . . to be informed

◇ **WORKBOOK:** Practices 21 and 22.

CHART 4-14: USING GERUNDS OR PASSIVE INFINITIVES FOLLOWING *NEED*

• British English can also use *want* in (c) and (d), but American English can use only *need* in those cases. For example: *The fence wants painting.*

☐ **EXERCISE 30, p. 181.** *Using gerunds or passive infinitives following* need.

ANSWERS: **1.** to fix . . . fixing/to be fixed **2.** to be cleaned/cleaning . . . to clean **3.** changing/to be changed **4.** to be ironed/ironing **5.** to be repaired/repair(ing) [The noun *repair* could be used instead of the gerund *repairing*.] **6.** to take . . . to be straightened/straightening **7.** to be picked/picking **8.** washing/to be washed

---

CHART 4-15: USING A POSSESSIVE TO MODIFY A GERUND

• This is another example of change in the English language. Formal usage keeps the traditional possessive form of the noun or pronoun before a gerund. Less formal usage permits the objective form.

☐ **EXERCISE 31, p. 182.** *Using a possessive to modify a gerund.*

This could be done in small groups, but it's probably more beneficial for the whole class to discuss the difference between formal and informal usage.

ANSWERS: **3.** We greatly appreciate your having taken/your taking the time to help us. **4. formal:** The boy resented our talking . . . . **informal:** . . . us talking . . . . **5.** Their running away/Their having run away . . . shocked everyone. **6. formal:** I don't understand your not wanting to do it. **informal:** . . . you not wanting . . . . **7. formal:** Sally complained about Ann's borrowing/having borrowed her clothes . . . . **informal:** . . . Ann borrowing her clothes . . . . **8. formal:** We should take advantage of Helen's being here . . . . **informal:** . . . of Helen being here . . . .

◇ **WORKBOOK:** Practice 23.

□ **EXERCISE 32, p. 182.** *Review of Charts 4-1 through 4-15.*

This exercise is quite long, so you might want to lead the class through it quickly. It takes about 10 minutes if the students are prepared.

ANSWERS: **1.** to be asked **2.** drinking [possible in British English: *to drink*] **3.** washing **4.** (in order) to relax **5.** to answer **6.** telling **7.** beating ["beat your head against a brick wall" = try to do something that is impossible] **8.** not being able **9.** to be awarded **10.** to accept **11.** getting . . . (in order) to help **12.** to travel . . . (to) leave **13.** Helping **14.** to be liked . . . (to be) trusted **15.** wondering **16.** to have been chosen **17.** Living **18.** doing . . . to interrupt **19.** to take/to have taken **20.** (in order) to let **21.** to cooperate **22.** to turn **23.** hearing/having heard **24.** leaving/having left . . . going/(having) gone . . . (in order) to study **25.** asking/having asked **26.** driving . . . to drive **27.** (in order) to get **28.** not being/not having been

◇ **WORKBOOK:** Practices 24 and 25.

CHART 4-16: USING VERBS OF PERCEPTION

- "Verbs of perception" refer to four of the five senses: sight, hearing, touch, smell (but not taste).

- Additional examples:
  (e) The cat **watched** the bird **fly** away. (The bird disappeared.)
  (f) The cat hungrily **watched** the bird **flying** above its head. (The bird continued to fly near the cat.)

- The "simple form" of a verb is the form that is usually listed in a dictionary, the form with no tense or endings. SIMPLE VERB: *go, accept* SIMPLE INFINITIVE: *to go, to accept*

□ **EXERCISE 33, p. 185.** *Understanding verbs of perception.*

Students can have fun demonstrating some of the situations in the entries, as if performing in a theater. Other students can describe the situation. For example, Carlos acts out being in an earthquake. Another student reports: "Carlos could feel the ground shake/shaking."

ANSWERS: **2.** shake/shaking **3.** ring/ringing **4.** sing/singing **5.** come/coming **6.** knock/knocking **7.** look at/looking at **8.** take off/taking off . . . land/landing [Use the same form for both verbs.] **11.** walking [in progress at this moment] **12.** walk . . . open . . . get in [Each step in the process was completed, not continuing.] **13.** walking [in progress as I watched] **14.** calling [in progress at this moment] **15.** call [He said my name one time, not over and over.] **16.** singing . . . laughing [continuing] **17.** burning [in progress at this moment] **18.** land [a single action, not continuing or repeated]

◇ **WORKBOOK:** Practices 26 and 27.

CHART 4-17: USING THE SIMPLE FORM AFTER *LET* AND **_HELP_**

- The American English preference is (c), the simple form of a verb rather than an infinitive after *help*. The British English preference is (d), the infinitive after *help*.

☐ **EXERCISE 34, p. 186.** *Using the simple form after* let *and* help.

The purpose is to accustom the students to using simple forms after *let* and *help*. If additional practice is needed, you and the students can think of new sentences. The *Workbook* also has more items in Practices 28 and 29.

ANSWERS: [Depend on students' creativity.]

CHART 4-18: USING CAUSATIVE VERBS: *MAKE, HAVE, GET*

• A ''causative'' verb carries the meaning that something/someone produces (causes) a result. This may be a difficult concept in some cultures, and languages express the notion of causation in very different ways. Therefore, you may need to discuss causation with your students.

• The method of causation is expressed by choosing one of the three verbs: *make* = use force; *have* = request or order; *get* = use persuasion or perhaps trickery.

☐ **EXERCISE 35, p. 187.** *Understanding causative verbs.*

Each response should perhaps be discussed so that students understand (1) the verb form and (2) the meaning of the causative verb.

ANSWERS: **3.** write **4.** wash **5.** to clean **6.** cashed [passive: by whom?] **7.** to go **8.** shortened [passive: by whom?] **9.** redo [redo = do again, pronounced /riy-**du**/] **10.** filled **11.** to lend **12.** removed **13.** cry [*Peeling*, a gerund, is the subject, so the verb *makes* ends in -s.] **14.** to do **15.** take **16.** cleaned [by whom?]

☐ **EXERCISE 36, p. 188.** *Using causative verbs.*

ANSWERS: [Depend on students' ideas.]

◇ **WORKBOOK:** Practices 28 and 29.

**CHART 4-19: SPECIAL EXPRESSIONS FOLLOWED BY THE
-ING FORM OF A VERB**

• In (c) through (g), you might substitute other expressions of time, money, and place that are more familiar to your students. For example:

(c) Jose *spends **five hours a day** studying* English.
(d) Yoko *wasted **fifty yen** riding* the bus.

The students can probably think of other good examples, too.

• Additional examples for (h) and (i):

(h) When Tom got home, he **found** his wife **crying** over a broken vase.
Looking for my glasses, I **found** them **sitting** on my nose.
(i) During the exam, the teacher **caught** a student **cheating.**
Judy **caught** her sister **wearing** her favorite jeans.

☐ **EXERCISE 37, p. 189.** *Special expressions followed by -ing verbs.*

ANSWERS: **2.** understanding **3.** doing **4.** waiting **5.** taking **6.** going/driving/riding/traveling, etc. **7.** listening **8.** going **9.** getting **10.** making **11.** watching **12.** eating **13.** A: doing/getting.... B: [Depends on students' ideas.] **14.** through **16.** [Depend on students' creativity.]

◇ **WORKBOOK:** Practice 30.

☐ **EXERCISES 38 & 39, pp. 190–194.** *General review of Chapter 4.*

There are plenty of items in these exercises for additional practice of all the material in Chapter 4. You might do a few with the whole class, then let them do the rest in small groups. After enough time, discuss only those items which caused difficulty. Again, see the INTRODUCTION, pp. xv–xvi, for various ways of using fill-in-the-blanks exercises.

EX. 38 ANSWERS: **1.** looking **2.** make **3.** watching...swim/swimming **4.** to pay **5.** to ignore **6.** studying **7.** feel **8.** draw **9.** laugh **10.** convincing **11.** open **12.** trickling/trickle **13.** filled [passive] **14.** telling **15.** being elected **16.** lying [Check the spelling.] **17.** (to) move **18.** play...joining **19.** drink [This is a folk saying. It means that you cannot always persuade a person to do what is reasonable.] **20.** play **21.** to be... (to) listen **22.** thinking **23.** taken **24.** to be told [by you] **25.** have...join **26.** being...being **27.** understanding **28.** tear ["tear my hair out" = feel frustration or anger] **29.** doing **30.** drive

EX. 39 ANSWERS:

1. take
2. translate
3. to say...understand
4. to begin
5. to be done [by someone]
6. to discover
7. put
8. feel...to be intimidated
9. failing
10. twiddling ["twiddling your thumbs" = doing nothing]
11. (in order) to let...run
12. make
13. talking
14. being
15. going
16. being/to be forced to leave...(in order) to study...having
17. to have...to know
18. Looking...realize...to be
19. sipping...eating
20. being
21. staying...getting
22. to force...to use...to feel...(to) share
23. sleeping
24. having...adjusting
25. to be admitted
26. to get...cut...trimmed

◇ **WORKBOOK:** Practices 31, 32, 33, 34, 35.

☐ **EXERCISE 40, p. 194.** *Review of Chapter 4.*

ANSWERS:
1. My parents made me [no *to*] promise to write them once a week.
2. I don't mind **having** a roommate.
3. Most students want **to** return home as soon as possible.
4. When I went [no *to*] shopping last Saturday, I saw a man [no *to*] drive his car....
5. I asked my roommate to let me [no *to*] use his shoe polish.
6. It is very interesting to learn about another country. OR Learning/To learn about another country is very interesting.
7. I don't enjoy **playing** card games.
8. I heard a car door **open and close/opening and closing** [*Open and close* = once; *opening and closing* = repeatedly. Both words should be in parallel form.]

9. I had my friend [no *to*] lend me his car.
10. I tried very hard ***not to*** make any mistakes.
11. It is ***very*** beautiful.
12. The music director tapped his baton ***(in order) to begin*** the rehearsal.
13. Some people prefer ***saving <u>their</u>*** money to ***spending*** it./Some people prefer ***to save their*** money ***<u>(rather) than (to) spend</u>*** it.
14. The task of ***finding*** a person . . . .
15. All of us needed to ***go*** to the cashier's window.
16. I am looking forward to ***going swimming*** in the ocean.
17. When ***you're/you are*** planting a garden, it's important to ***know*** about soils.
18. My mother always ***makes*** me [no *to be*] slow down if she ***thinks*** I am driving ***<u>too</u>*** fast.
19. One of our fights ended up with ***me/my*** having to ***be*** sent to the hospital ***for*** stitches/***(in order) to get*** stitches.

◇ **WORKBOOK:** Have students take Practice Test A and/or B.

☐ **EXERCISE 41, p. 195.** *Written composition.*

Students should be able to produce several informal paragraphs on a topic. After they finish, they or a partner might underline all the gerunds and infinitives.

All of the topics require use of more than one verb tense. Topic 1 is basically about the past but might also include the present perfect. Topic 2 combines the present and the past. Topic 3 requires the present and either present perfect or past.

It is not necessary for students to answer each question directly. These questions are designed to produce ideas or to recall memories which the students can write about.

☐ **EXERCISE 42, p. 195.** *Using phrasal verbs.*

(See Appendix 2 for lists of phrasal verbs.)

ANSWERS: **1.** up **2.** in . . . over **3.** up **4.** after **5.** up **6.** out **7.** up **8.** down **9.** up **10.** out

Appendix 1: SUPPLEMENTARY GRAMMAR UNITS

Unit A: Basic Grammar Terminology
Unit B: Questions
Unit C: Negatives
Unit D: Articles

General Notes on Appendix 1:

• PURPOSES: Teachers and students need a common vocabulary of grammar terms so that they can identify and discuss the patterns they are using in English. Also, every language learner needs to use a dictionary, and every dictionary uses grammar terms. Appendix 1 presents basic terms and patterns with some short exercises for clarification of chart information and a few longer ones for practice.

• USES: At the beginning of the English course, you could show your students the appendices and suggest how to use them. Also refer them to the Selfstudy Practices in the *Workbook*. The textbook assumes that your students are already familiar with basic grammar terminology, but often it is helpful for them to review these concepts, either on their own or at your direction. You may want to cover some of the Appendix 1 units in connection with related units in the chapter material.

Unit A: Basic Grammar Terminology

CHART A-1: SUBJECTS, VERBS, AND OBJECTS

• Write simple sentences on the board and have the students identify subjects, verbs, and objects until you're satisfied that this basic grammar is thoroughly understood by all.

• Some common verbs that are usually or always intransitive: *agree, appear, arrive, come, cost, cry, die, exist, fall, flow, go, happen, laugh, live, occur, rain, rise, seem, sit, sleep, sneeze, snow, stand, stay, talk, wait, walk.*

• Not all languages employ the same categories of grammar in the same ways. For example, the verb *enjoy* must always be transitive in English, but in some languages its equivalent is intransitive. (A good dictionary identifies each verb as transitive or intransitive.)

TRANSITIVE:
$$\begin{array}{lll} \textbf{S} & \textbf{V} & \textbf{O} \\ \textit{I enjoyed} & \textit{the party} & \textit{very much.} \end{array}$$

$$\begin{array}{lll} \textbf{S} & \textbf{V} & \textbf{O} \\ \textit{I enjoyed} & \textit{myself} & \textit{at the party.} \end{array}$$

INTRANSITIVE: [*I enjoyed very much.* = ungrammatical English]

• Have the students look in their dictionaries to find the abbreviated labels **n, v, vi, vt, adj, adv, prep.** (Warn them that not all dictionaries use the same abbreviations.)

◇ **WORKBOOK:** Practices 1 and 2.

CHART A-2: PREPOSITIONS AND PREPOSITIONAL PHRASES

• A preposition is a kind of "cement" that connects a noun or pronoun to the other parts of an English sentence. Many languages have no prepositions, so these small English words can be very difficult to understand and explain. To get across the importance of these words, take a simple sentence such as "I walked ____ my father" and complete it with as many different prepositions as possible: *I walked with, toward, into, beside, behind, like, on (!), under (?), around (etc.) my father.*

• In (d) notice that a comma is customary before the subject of the sentence. This comma signals that an element has been moved to the front of the sentence, and the speaker's voice will rise a bit before the comma.

• A few prepositions consist of short phrases; for example:

because of	*in the middle of*	*out of*
instead of	*in (the) back of*	*according to*
in (the) front of	*ahead of*	*due to*

◇ **WORKBOOK:** Practices 3 and 4.

☐ **EXERCISE 1, p. A2.** *Identifying subjects, verbs, objects, and prepositions.*

Most students should be able to identify each structure quickly. If not, perhaps they need to review a more basic English textbook. Only #6 is intended to be at all challenging.

ANSWERS:

           S   **V**   **PP**
2. The children walked   to school.
         S   **V**   **O**
3. Beethoven wrote   nine symphonies. [*Nine* is an adjective here.]
   S   **V**   **O**   **PP**
4. Mary did   her homework   at the library. [*Her* is a possessive adjective here (see p. A6).]
   S   **V**   **PP**
5. Bells originated   in Asia.
            S   **V**   **O**   **PP**
6. Chinese printers created   the first paper money   in the world.
   [*Chinese* = an adjective here.]
   [*the first* = an ordinal or counting expression.]
   [*paper* = a noun adjunct (a noun that modifies the next noun); see Chart 5-4 in Chapter 5.]

CHART A-3: ADJECTIVES and CHART A-4: ADVERBS

• Have the class call out words they think are adjectives and make sentences with these words.

• In general, adjectives are placed before nouns in English.

• Another common pattern places an adjective after the verb *be* or other linking verbs. (See Charts A-5 and A-6.)
   (a) *The student is intelligent.*
   (b) *The children were hungry.*

• Chart A-4 summarizes only the basic form and placement of adverbs. There are many other phenomena related to adverbs, but they are not included here.

◇ **WORKBOOK:** Practices 5, 6, 7.

□ EXERCISES 2 & 3, pp. A3–A4. *Adjectives and adverbs.*

EX. 2 ANSWERS: **1.** careless . . . carelessly **2.** easy . . . easily **3.** softly . . . soft **4.** quietly **5.** well . . . good

EX. 3 ANSWERS: **2.** Chinese [adj.] . . . beautiful [adj.] **3.** old [adj.] . . . wooden [adj.] . . . skillfully [adv.] **4.** busy [adj.] . . . usually [midsentence frequency adv.] . . . short [adj.] **5.** young [adj.] . . . very [adv.] good [adj.] . . . yesterday [adv.] [Note: Prepositional phrases *from jade* (item 2) and *on the telephone* (item 4) might also be called adverbial expressions.]

□ EXERCISE 4, p. A4. *Midsentence adverbs.*

Ask the students to use these adverbs in their usual positions. Point out that using them in other positions is possible and focuses attention on them; e.g., **Never** *has Erica seen snow.* (See Chart C-3.) **Often** *Ted studies at the library in the evening. Ann* **often** *is at the library in the evening, too. Fred has finished studying for tomorrow's test* **already.**

ANSWERS: **2.** Ted often studies . . . . **3.** Ann is often at the library . . . . **4.** Fred has already finished . . . . **5.** Jack is seldom at home. **6.** Does he always stay here? **7.** He often goes . . . [*hang around* = enjoy idle time, leisure; *buddies* = close friends, pals, mates] **8.** You should always tell the truth.

CHART A-5: THE VERB *BE* and CHART A-6: LINKING VERBS

- Some grammar books call *be* a linking verb.

- It is important for learners to understand that *be* can function in two ways:
  —as the main verb in a sentence (a, b, c)
  —as the auxiliary element in a verb phrase (d, e, f)

□ EXERCISE 5, p. A5. *Adjectives and adverbs.*

ANSWERS: **1.** easy . . . easily **2.** comfortable **3.** carefully **4.** sad **5.** cheerfully . . . cheerful **6.** carefully . . . good [*The soup tasted good* = it had a delicious flavor.] **7.** quiet [*got* = became] . . . quietly **8.** dark [*grew* = became]

◇ **WORKBOOK:** Practices 8, 9, 10.

CHART A-7: PERSONAL PRONOUNS

- The use of apostrophes can be a problem for second language learners as well as for native speakers of English. Call attention to the note below the chart.

- The "antecedent" may also be called the "referent."

- The term "possessive adjective" is useful to distinguish *my* from *mine*, but a "possessive adjective" is still a "pronoun." The terminology is awkward.

◇ **WORKBOOK:** Practices 11 and 12.

☐ **EXERCISE 6, p. A6.** *Pronouns and antecedents.*

ANSWERS: **2.** *they* (pronoun): monkeys (antecedent)   **3.** *She*: teacher... *them*: papers
4. *It*: cormorant... *it*: cormorant... *them*: fishermen [Note that the antecedent for *it* is not "a
diving bird"; *it* refers specifically to "the cormorant," for it is not true that any diving bird is able
to stay under water for a long time. And it is the cormorant, not "a diving bird," that is used to
catch fish for fishermen.] [Your students might be interested in how English has changed
recently: *policeman* has become *police officer*, *fireman* has become *firefighter*, *mailman* has become
letter carrier. *Fisherman* has not yet developed a widely accepted alternative expression, but some
people use *fisherperson*.]   **5.** *him*: Tom... *He*: Tom... *it*: apple

☐ **EXERCISE 7, p. A6.** *Possessive pronouns and possessive adjectives.*

ANSWERS: **1.** my....   **2.** mine...yours   **3.** their...hers   **4.** its   **5.** It's (It is)...
its...its   **6.** Its...It's (It is)...It's (It has)

CHART A-8: CONTRACTIONS

• This chart is useful with Chapter 1: Verb Tenses.

• Make sure the students understand that the contractions in quotation marks are NOT written.

• Mention the possibility that learners may have difficulty with auxiliary verbs in their own speech and
writing because they don't always hear them in normal, rapid spoken English. Unstressed contracted
forms may be barely discernible to the inexperienced, unaware ear.

◇ **WORKBOOK:** Practice 13.

☐ **EXERCISE 8, p. A7.** *Contractions.*

Have the students listen carefully to your oral production. Students enjoy trying to copy the
teacher's model, but the emphasis should be on their <u>hearing</u> the contractions you say.

ANSWERS: **1.** My *friend's* here.   **2.** My *friends're* here.   **3.** *Tom's* /tamz/ been   **4.** The
students've /studəntsəv/   **5.** *Bob'd* /"Bob"-əd/   **6.** Bob'd   **7.** *Don'll*/"Don"-əl/   **8.** The
window's /windouz/ open.   **9.** The *windows're* /windouzər/ open.   **10.** *Jane's* never....
11. *boys've* /boizəv/   **12.** *Sally'd* /sælid/ forgotten   **13.** *Sally'd* forget   **14.** *Who's* /hu:z/ that
woman?   **15.** *Who're* /huər/ those people?   **16.** *Who's* been taking   **17.** *What've* /hwətəv/
you been doing   **18.** *What'd* /hwətəd/ you been doing   **19.** *What'd* you like....
20. *What'd* you do....   **21.** *Why'd* /hwaid/ you stay   **22.** *When'll* /hwenəl/ I see you again?
23. How *long'll* /lɔŋəl/ you   **24.** *Where'm* /hwɛrəm/ I   **25.** *Where'd* /hwɛrd/ you stay?

Unit B: Questions

Every chapter in the textbook requires students not only to understand but to produce question
forms. Students need to be able to ask and answer them grammatically. Even advanced students
can profit from review. Unit B can be a useful lesson with Chapter 1 (Verb Tenses) and/or Chapter
7 (Noun Clauses). It can also be allotted its own slot in a syllabus.

CHART B-1: FORMS OF YES/NO AND INFORMATION QUESTIONS

- The chart gives a statement of fact—(a) to (k)—on the left. In the center are two forms of questions about that given fact. On the right are notes about word forms and order, the main points of difficulty for learners of English.

- To reinforce the word order, you might copy the center of the chart on the chalkboard. Students can look there instead of in their books as they do the exercises, and you can point to the correct position for each word.

- Note the special form of questions with *who* as subject.

◇ **WORKBOOK:** Practice 14.

☐ **EXERCISE 9, p. A9.** *Forming questions.*

The purpose of this mechanical exercise is for students to review the word order of questions using a variety of verb forms.

SUGGESTION: Draw a chart on the chalkboard with the following headings:

Q Word + Auxiliary + Subject + Main Verb + Rest of the Sentence

Then ask students to fit each element of a question sentence into the chart. This makes clear the position of each element in a question. For example:

Q Word +	Auxiliary +	Subject +	Main Verb +	Rest of the Sentence
	Does	she	stay	there?
Where	does	she	stay?	

As a variation, you could divide the class into thirds. Group 1 reads the cue, Group 2 asks the yes/no question, then Group 3 asks the information question. You could have four groups, with Group 4 asking the question with *who*. Rotate the groups occasionally so that everyone has a chance to use each question type. The exercise is mechanical, but it can be turned into a game.

ANSWERS: [all three types]
1. Does she stay there? Where does she stay? Who stays there?
2. Is she staying there? Where is she staying? Who is staying there?
3. Will she stay there? Where will she stay? Who will stay there?
4. Is she going to stay there? Where is she going to stay? Who is going to stay there?
5. Did they stay there? Where did they stay? Who stayed there?
6. Will they be staying there? Where will they be staying? Who will be staying there?
7. Should they stay there? Where should they stay? Who should stay there?
8. Has he stayed there? Where has he stayed? Who has stayed there?
9. Has he been staying there? Where has he been staying? Who has been staying there?
10. Is John there? Where is John? Who is there?
11. Will John be there? Where will John be? Who will be there?
12. Has John been there? Where has John been? Who has been there?
13. Will Judy have been there? Where will Judy have been? Who will have been there?
14. Were Ann and Tom married there? Where were . . . ? Who was married there?
15. Should this package have been taken there? Where should this . . . ? What should have . . . ?

• This chart is for consolidation and review. It is intended for reference, not memorization. In order to acquaint the students with its contents, spend a little time discussing it in class, including modeling spoken contractions (e.g., *When'd they arrive?*). After you discuss it, have the students close their books. Give answers from the ANSWER column (adapting them to your class), and have the students supply possible questions. Examples:

> TEACHER: David's. [OR Yoko's, Olga's, Ali's, Roberto's, etc.]
> STUDENT: Whose . . . ?
> TEACHER: Yesterday.
> STUDENT: When . . . ?
> TEACHER: Dark brown.
> STUDENT: What color . . . ?

◇ **WORKBOOK:** Practices 15, 16, 17, 18, 19, 20, 21.

☐ **EXERCISES 10 → 12, pp. A12–A13.** *Forming information questions.*

Of course, changing a statement into a question is not part of normal communication. Nevertheless, learners need to understand the grammatical relationships between statements and questions. These exercises practice those relationships.

To make the exercise more like a dialogue, you could follow this pattern:

1. TEACHER (to STUDENT B): You need five dollars.
   STUDENT A to B: How much money do you need?
   STUDENT B to A: I need five dollars.

2. TEACHER (to STUDENT D): (. . .) was born in (. . .). [Use real information.]
   STUDENT C to D: Where was (. . .) born?
   STUDENT D to C: S/He was born in (. . .).

EX. 10 ANSWERS: **2.** Where was Roberto born? / In what country/city was . . . ? / What country/city was Roberto born in? **3.** How often do you go out to eat? **4.** Who(m) are you waiting for? [*For whom are you waiting?* is very formal and seldom used.] **5.** Who answered the phone? **6.** Who(m) did you call? **7.** Who called? **8.** What does the boy have in his pocket? [British: *What has the boy (got) in his pocket?*] **9.** What does "deceitful" mean? **10.** What is an abyss? **11.** Which way did he go? **12.** Whose books and papers are these? **13.** How many children do they have? [British or regional American: *How many children have they?*] **14.** How long has he been here? **15.** How far is it/How many miles is it to New Orleans? ["New Orleans" has at least two commonly used pronunciations. Whatever pronunciation your students are familiar with is correct.]

EX. 11 ANSWERS: **1.** How much gas/How many gallons of gas/What did she buy? [In British English, gas = *petrol*.] **2.** When/At what time can the doctor see me? **3.** Who **is** her roommate? **4.** Who **are** her roommates? **5.** How long/How many years have your parents been living there? **6.** Whose book is this? **7.** What made her sneeze? **8.** Who's coming over for dinner? **9.** What color **is** Ann's dress? **10.** What color **are** Ann's eyes? **11.** Why **were you** late? / How come **you were** late? **12.** Who can't go . . . ? **13.** Why **can't Bob** go? / How come **Bob can't** go? **14.** Why **didn't you**/ How come **you didn't** answer . . . ? [formal and rare: *Why **did you not** answer the phone?*] **15.** What kind of music do you like? **16.** What don't you understand? **17.** What **is** Janet **doing** right now? **18.** How do you spell "sitting"? [*you* = impersonal pronoun] **19.** What **does** Tom **look like**? **20.** What **is** Tom **like**? **21.** What does Ron do (for a living)? **22.** How far/How many miles is Mexico from here? **23.** How do you take/like your coffee? **24.** Which (city) is farther north, Stockholm or Moscow? / Of Stockholm and Moscow, which (city/one) is farther north? **25.** How are you getting along?

EX. 12 ANSWERS: [There is more than one possible response to most items.]
1. How far/How many miles is it to (...)? [Use a familiar place name.]
2. When does fall semester begin? / What begins on...?
3. Which pen did...?
4. Who typed...? / What did the secretary type?
5. How many courses did...?
6. What does ''rapid'' mean?
7. Who went...? / Where did (...) go?
8. Who telephoned you?
9. Where is the post office?
10. How far is it to...?
11. How long did you...? / How many hours did you...?
12. Who gave a speech? / What did (...) do?
13. & 14. Who talked about...? / What did (...) talk about? / About what did (...) talk?
15. How much money / What do you need?
16. Which floor does (...) live on? / On which floor does (...) live?
17. Where will you be...?
18. Whose pen is this?
19. How often do you go to the library? / Where do you go every day?
20. When / On what day is...?
21. How long have you been...?
22. Why did you laugh?
23. Who dropped...?
24. Who(m) should I give this book to? / To whom should I...?
25. Why didn't you come... / How come you didn't come...?

□ **EXERCISE 13, p. A13.** *Forming questions.*

Many items in this exercise could become a dialogue in the following way:

TEACHER to STUDENT A: ''I had a sandwich for lunch.''
STUDENT A to STUDENT B: ''The teacher had a sandwich for lunch. What did *you* have?''
STUDENT B to STUDENT A: ''I had (...).''

TEACHER to STUDENT A: ''These are my books.''
STUDENT A to STUDENT B: ''These are the teacher's books. Whose are *those*?'' (pointing)
STUDENT B to STUDENT A: ''These are mine/my books/(...'s).''

ANSWERS: **1.** What did you have for lunch? **2.** Whose books are those? **3.** Which chapter are we supposed...? **4.** Who(m) did you talk to?/To whom did you talk? **5.** What did you talk to (...) about? **6.** Why did you fall asleep...? **7.** Who(m) does that book belong to?/To whom does that book belong? **8.** What does ''request'' mean? **9.** How far is it to (...)? **10.** How many languages can you speak? **11.** Who opened...? **12.** Why didn't you go...? **13.** Which house do you live in? **14.** Where did you hang...? **15.** Who(m) is the letter addressed to? / To whom is...? **16.** How long did it take (you) to finish your assignments? **17.** Where did Mr. Smith teach English? / What did...teach in Japan? / Who taught English in Japan? **18.** When/What time should I be here? [*be here* = arrive for an appointment.] **19.** Whose keys did you find? / What did you find? **20.** How often/How many times a year do you visit your aunt and uncle?

CHART B-3: NEGATIVE QUESTIONS

• Negative questions are seldom found in nonfiction writing (other than as rhetorical questions). They are principally conversational, expressing emotions and opinions.

• The speaker of a negative question has an opinion about a situation. Asking the negative question is a signal to the listener. The speaker expects a certain answer, but the listener has to answer truthfully. Sometimes, therefore, the answer is unexpected. Even with native speakers, this can cause confusion, so the questioner may have to ask another question for clarification. For example:

(e) A: "What happened? Didn't you study?"
    B: "Yes." [Meaning: "That is what happened." Speaker A had expected a "no" answer.]
    A: "I'm confused. Did you study or didn't you?"
    B: "No, I didn't."

◇ **WORKBOOK:** Practice 22.

☐ **EXERCISE 14, p. A15.** *Using negative questions.*

Because negative questions are quite confusing, you should probably lead the students through this exercise. Help them understand the situation and expectation in each item.

ANSWERS:

2. A. Wasn't she in class?
   B. No. [= No, she was not in class.]

3. A: Isn't that Mrs. Robbins?
   B: Yes (, it is).

4. A: Aren't you hungry?
   B. Yes (, I am).

5. A: Didn't you sleep well last night?
   B: No (, I didn't).

6. A: Don't you feel well?
   B: No (, I don't). /
      Yes (, that's the problem).

7. A: Doesn't the sun/it rise in the east?
   B: Yes . . . .

8. A: Don't you recognize him?
   B: No (, I don't).

CHART B-4: TAG QUESTIONS

• Tag questions are an important element in English language conversation. They help establish communication because they invite a response from another person. Using the questions incorrectly can, therefore, cause confusion and disrupt communication. Students should be aware of the importance of using tag questions correctly.

• Ask the students to make sentences beginning with "I'm not sure, but I think . . . ." Have them turn each statement of opinion into an inquiry with a tag question that indicates their belief. For example: *I'm not sure, but I think we're going to have a test on question forms tomorrow.* → *We're going to have a test on question forms tomorrow, aren't we?* Another example: *I'm not sure, but I think Venus is the second closest planet to the sun.* → *Venus is the second closest planet to the sun, isn't it?*

   To elicit negatives in the main rather than tag verb, have the students begin a sentence with "It is my understanding that . . . not . . . ." For example: *It is my understanding that we're not going to have a test tomorrow.* → *We're not going to have a test tomorrow, are we?*

• Asking questions without using question word order or tags is common in everyday speech: the speaker simply uses interrogative intonation (voice rising at end). Demonstrate for the students: *Mary isn't here? She'll be here at ten? They won't be here? You can't come? You've never been to Paris? You live with your parents?* etc.

◇ **WORKBOOK:** Practice 23.

☐ **EXERCISE 15, p. A16.** *Tag questions.*

> Most of the items here would typically have a rising intonation. Of course, some could be said with a falling intonation.
>
> *ANSWERS:* **2.** isn't she   **3.** will they   **4.** are there   **5.** isn't it   **6.** isn't he   **7.** hasn't he [*He's learned* = "he has learned"]   **8.** doesn't/hasn't he   **9.** can she   **10.** won't she **11.** wouldn't she   **12.** are they   **13.** have you   **14.** isn't it   **15.** can't they   **16.** did they **17.** did it   **18.** aren't I/am I not

☐ **EXERCISE 16, p. A17.** *Tag questions.*

> Perhaps you could tell the students which intonation to use for certain items. Or you could allow them to choose rising or falling intonation and then explain their choices. Or you could simply concentrate on the grammar and pay scant attention to intonation.
>
> *ANSWERS:* **1.** isn't it?   **2.** isn't he/she?   **3.** doesn't he/she?   **4.** is there?   **5.** doesn't he/she?   **6.** didn't you?   **7.** hasn't he/she?   **8.** did you?   **9.** have they?   **10.** don't they?   **11.** can he/she/they?   **12.** is he/she?   **13.** won't it?   **14.** do they?   **15.** didn't you?   **16.** isn't there?   **17.** isn't he/she?   **18.** shouldn't you?   **19.** does he/she? **20.** didn't he/she?   **21.** don't we?   **22.** haven't you?   **23.** won't he/she?   **24.** have they? [Traditionally, the pronoun *nobody* is singular. Some grammar books, therefore, insist on the traditional tag *has he.* Usage is changing toward a preference for the plural form, however.] **25.** aren't I?/am I not?   **26.** doesn't it?

Unit C: Negatives

┌───┐
│ **CHART C-1: USING *NOT* AND OTHER NEGATIVE WORDS**

• A note on pronunciation of some contractions:
  1. Do not pronounce the letter "l" in *could(n't), should(n't), would(n't).* They should sound like "good."
  2. Do not pronounce the first "t" in *mustn't.*
  3. Pronounce the letter "s" in *hasn't, isn't,* and *doesn't* like the letter "z."
└───┘

◇ **WORKBOOK:** Practice 24.

☐ **EXERCISE 17, p. A18.** *Using negative words.*

> The purpose of this exercise is to show students two equally correct ways to make a negative statement. The form with *no* is generally more formal. Caution students against double negatives.
>
> *ANSWERS:* **2.** There wasn't any food. / There was no food.   **3.** I didn't receive any... / I received no....   **4.** I don't need any help. / I need no help.   **5.** We don't have any... / We have no....   **6.** You shouldn't have given the beggar any money. [The other alternative is less likely: *You should have given the beggar no money.*]   **7.** I don't trust anyone. / I trust no one. **8.** I didn't see anyone. / I saw no one.   **9.** There wasn't anyone... / There was no one.... **10.** She can't find anybody... / She can find no one....

CHART C-2: AVOIDING "DOUBLE NEGATIVES"

• Some native speakers of English use double negatives regularly in their speech, so students might hear double negatives and wonder if they are grammatical. Double negatives are considered to be nonstandard usage and may reflect disadvantageously on one's educational background. However, they are sometimes used for a humorous or theatrical effect.

◇ WORKBOOK: Practice 25.

☐ EXERCISE 18, p. A19. *Avoiding double negatives.*

> *ANSWERS:*
> 1. I *don't* need *any help.* / I *need no* help.
> 2. I *didn't* see *anybody.* / I *saw nobody.*
> 3. I *can never* ... / I *can't ever* understand him.
> 4. He *doesn't* like *either* coffee *or* tea. / He *likes neither* coffee *nor* tea.
> 5. I *didn't* do *anything.* / I *did nothing.*
> 6. I *can hardly* hear... [*hardly* is a negative word]
> 7. We *couldn't* see *anything* ... / We *could see nothing* but sand.
> 8. ... *have barely* changed (at all) ... / ... *haven't changed* at all ...

CHART C-3: BEGINNING A SENTENCE WITH A NEGATIVE WORD

• This inversion is principally a literary device. Advanced students may find it interesting. Intermediate students may well ignore it.

◇ WORKBOOK: Practice 26.

☐ EXERCISE 19, p. A19. *Word order with negative words.*

> *ANSWERS:* **2.** Seldom do I sleep .... **3.** Hardly ever do I agree with her. **4.** Never will I forget .... **5.** Never have I known Pat .... **6.** Scarcely ever does the mail arrive .... [no "s" with *arrive* because the "s" is with *does*]

Unit D: Articles

CHARTS D-1 and D-2: BASIC ARTICLE USAGE

• Articles are very difficult for students to understand and use correctly. Many languages do not have articles. Languages that do have articles use them differently from English. Articles are, in many teachers' experiences, difficult to teach. There are many nuances, complex patterns of use, and idiomatic variations. Students who are frustrated trying to understand and use articles should be reminded that articles are just a small component of English. Proficiency in using articles improves with experience; it cannot be assured overnight by learning "rules."

• The exercises point out some contrasts in usage that should help the students understand the differences among *a/an*, *the*, and the absence of any article (symbolized by Ø).

• Note the reference to Chart 5-8 in section II of Chart D-1. Chapter 5 (in Volume B) is a good place to use this unit to cover the basic uses of articles. If you are using only Book A, you might use this unit on articles at any time, and then periodically discuss the usage of articles in exercises and in the students' oral/written reponses.

• Some students may need a reminder about using *an* instead of *a*. English speakers prefer not to pronounce a vowel sound after the article *a*. Therefore, they put *n* between the two vowel sounds. For example:

a + apple → an apple; a + old man → an old man; a + umbrella → an umbrella
[But note that *a university* has no *n* because the *u* begins with a sort of *y* or consonant sound.]
Also:
a + other → another [Tradition causes this to be written as one word.]

◇ **WORKBOOK:** Practices 27 and 28.

☐ **EXERCISES 20 & 21, pp. A21—A23.** *Using articles.*

Exercise 20 is a series of dialogues. Students can work in pairs or two students can read one dialogue to the whole class.

EX. 20 ANSWERS: **3.** *a* good reason **4.** *the* reason [Both people know Jack's specific reason. Now they are deciding whether to believe it or not.] **5.** *the* washing machine [Both people know the same machine.] . . . *a* different shirt [no specific shirt] **6.** *a* washing machine **7.** *The* front wheel . . . *a* parked car . . . *a* big pothole . . . *the* car [Now both people know about the same specific car.] . . . *a* note . . . *the* owner [Each car usually has only one owner.] . . . *the* car . . . *the* note [Now both people know about this note.] . . . *an* apology **8.** *The* radiator [Each car has only one radiator.] . . . *a* leak . . . *the* windshield wipers . . . *the* leak **9.** *the* closet . . . *the* front hallway [specific locations that both people are familiar with]

EX. 21 ANSWERS: **4.** Ø hats [no article] **5.** *A* hat . . . *an* article **6.** Ø Hats . . . Ø articles **7.** *The* brown hat **8.** Ø problems . . . Ø life **9.** *a* long life **10.** *the* life [Note the difference between item 9 and item 10.] **11.** *an* engineer **12.** *an* engineer **13.** *the* name . . . *the* engineer . . . *an* infection . . . *the* bridge **14.** Ø people . . . Ø jewelry **15.** *The* jewelry **16.** *a* beautiful ring . . . Ø gold . . . Ø rubies . . *The* gold [Now it's familiar, specific.] . . . *The* rubies . . . **17.** *a* new city . . . *a* place . . . Ø newspapers . . . Ø advertisements . . . Ø apartments . . . *an* ad . . . *a* furnished apartment, *the* apartment . . . *a* stove . . . *a* refrigerator . . . Ø furniture . . . Ø beds . . . Ø tables . . . Ø chairs . . . *a* sofa. **18.** *a* short time . . . *a* furnished apartment . . . *The* apartment . . . *a* good location . . . *the* stove . . . *The* refrigerator . . . *the* refrigerator door . . . *The* bed . . . *the* furniture . . . Ø another apartment [*another = an + other*]

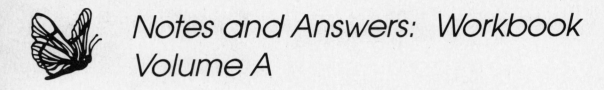

Notes and Answers: Workbook Volume A

This *Guide* includes the answers only to the Guided Study Practices in the *Workbook*. (The answers to the Selfstudy Practices are in the back of the student's workbook.) In many of the Guided Study Practices, the answers depend upon the students' creativity, so no answers can be supplied here.

Chapter 1: VERB TENSES

◇ **PRACTICE 7, p. 8:** *The simple present and the present progressive.*

1. usually drinks . . . is drinking   **2.** takes . . . usually waits   **3.** is raining . . . is standing . . . is holding . . . is waiting   **4.** is taking . . . studies . . . has . . . is also taking . . . likes . . . has   **5.** are you doing . . . am tasting . . . tastes   **6.** are you writing . . . am making . . . Do you always prepare . . . always try   **7.** is always interrupting/always interrupts . . . is always asking/always asks   **8.** am preparing . . . don't need

◇ **PRACTICE 8, p. 10:** *Irregular verbs.*

In this exercise, the irregular verbs are grouped according to similarity of form. It is assumed that the students already know most of these irregular verbs. They can infer the forms of verbs new to their vocabulary by associating them with ones they already know.

The students can use this exercise as a worksheet, possibly in preparation for a quiz. They can check their own or each other's answers by referring to Chart 1-11 in the main text, or they can ask you to quickly check over their answers. Tell them to pay careful attention to spelling.

◇ **PRACTICE 13, p. 15:** *Simple past of irregular verbs.*

[Answers depend upon students' creativity.] Verb forms:
1. wept   **2.** spun   **3.** sought   **4.** shed   **5.** shook   **6.** spread   **7.** fled   **8.** split
9. crept   **10.** clung   **11.** chose   **12.** sank

◇ **PRACTICE 16, p. 17:** *The simple past and the past progressive.*

2. was . . . was humming   **3.** were in our living room watching . . . went . . . went . . . got . . . turned . . . listened . . . was   **4.** outwitted [= outsmarted, were more clever] . . . surrounded . . . was still inside stuffing   **5.** rang . . . came . . . were still playing . . . was pulling . . . ran . . . told   **6.** was looking . . . Did you find . . . took

◇ **PRACTICE 17, p. 18:** *The simple past and the past progressive.*

Expected answers:
2. took/withdrew . . . bought/purchased . . . was driving . . . collided with/hit . . . demolished/destroyed/wrecked **3.** woke/got . . . heard . . . was walking/running/crawling **4.** visited/called on . . . were doing/were washing . . . came/knocked/arrived . . . finished . . . sat . . . talked/chatted/reminisced **5.** got to/arrived at . . . was waiting/was watching . . . saw . . . waved/raised . . . said/shouted . . . were making **6.** was . . . watering/sprinkling/tending . . . began/started . . . shut/turned

◇ **PRACTICE 21, p. 21:** *The present perfect.*

You might want to give students some limit on the length of—or amount of detail in—their written answers. A lengthy or detailed answer will require use of the simple past as well as the present perfect and could serve as practice in using both tenses. In evaluating the answers, reward each correct use of the present perfect. You might choose simply to note misspellings and other errors without focusing on them.

In preparation for (or possibly instead of) writing their answers, students could discuss them in small groups. Each member of the group could give an answer as the rest of the group listens for the use of the present perfect. At the end of the speaker's answer, the others could identify (orally or in writing) the present perfect verbs s/he used. As an alternative, the group could paraphrase (orally or in writing) what the speaker said, copying or correcting the speaker's use of tenses.

Another alternative is to divide the class into five groups. Each group discusses one item. Each student writes a summary of everything that was said in his/her group or the leader of each group presents an oral summary to the rest of the class. (You might want to expand the scope of #3 to include ''Why?,'' ''Do you ever expect to do these things?,'' and ''What are some interesting and unusual things that you have done and want to do again?'')

◇ **PRACTICE 23, p. 22:** *The present perfect and the present perfect progressive.*

2. have met **3.** has been standing **4.** I have always wanted **5.** has been painting **6.** have been travel(l)ing **7.** has grown **8.** have already spent **9.** has been cooking **10.** have never heard **11.** have been waiting **12.** has been digging

◇ **PRACTICE 24, p. 23:** *Writing.*

You might want to set some limit on the length of the students' answers, which could vary from a six-sentence paragraph to a 500-word narrative.

◇ **PRACTICE 27, p. 26:** *The past perfect.*

In these sentences, point out that the earlier or first action is in the past perfect and the later or second action is in the simple past.
[Answers depend on students' creativity.] Suggestions:
1. I had never [past participle] . . . before I [simple past tense verb] . . . .
2. By the time [subject + simple past] . . . , he had already [past participle] . . . .
3. In 1987, I [simple/progressive past] . . . . Prior to that time, I had [*been* + present participle] . . . .
4. When I [simple past] . . . , someone else had already [past participle] . . . .
5. Last January, I [simple past] . . . . Before that, I had never [past participle] . . . .
6. I had never [past participle] . . . until I [simple past] . . . .
7. The movie had [past participle] . . . by the time we [simple past] . . . .
8. My [subject + simple past verb] . . . after I had already [past participle] . . . .

◇ **PRACTICE 29, p. 27:** *Writing.*

You might want to set a limit on the length of the students' answers. When you evaluate their work, reward each correct use of verb tenses. You may choose not to pay much attention to mistakes in other areas, such as spelling and word choice, in order to keep the focus on verb tenses.

◇ **PRACTICE 31, p. 28:** Will *vs.* be going to.

1. I'll ["VCR" = video cassette recorder]   2. I'm going to   3. is going to . . . is he going to/will he   4. I'll   5. I'm going to . . . I'll   6. I'm going to   7. I'll [*c'mon* = "come on" = Be serious/realistic!]   8. I'll

◇ **PRACTICE 34, p. 30:** *Expressing the future in time clauses.*

The main point to remember is that a time clause (an adverb clause that begins with a time word like *after*, *until*, and *as soon as*) cannot contain a future verb form. If the students write out the sentences, have them underline the verbs.

◇ **PRACTICE 36, p. 31:** *Using the present progressive to express future time.*

Discuss situations in which the present progressive can be used to indicate future time.
3. I'm having   4. are you doing . . . I'm studying   5. [No change: *I'm getting it* would have a present, not future, meaning.]   6. are they getting   7. [No change: *You're laughing* is not a "planned event."]   8. we're moving   9. Is he teaching   10. I'm not sending . . . are coming

◇ **PRACTICE 39, p. 33:** *Past and future.*

Suggest that the students use *will*; forms of *be going to* are also possible.
2. He'll shave and shower and then make
3. After he eats . . . , he'll get
4. By the time he gets . . . , he'll have drunk
5. . . . he'll dictate . . . and plan
6. . . . he'll have finished
7. . . . he'll be attending
8. He'll go . . . and have
9. After he finishes . . . , he'll take . . . before he returns
10. He'll work . . . until he goes
11. . . . he leaves . . . , he will have attended
12. . . . gets . . . will be playing
13. . . . will have been playing
14. finishes . . . , he'll take
15. will sit . . . and discuss
16. They'll watch . . . will put
17. he goes . . . Dick will have had . . . will be ready

◇ **PRACTICE 42, p. 35:** *Review of tenses.*

I. 2. I've been looking   3. is seeing [= is meeting with]   4. received   5. sounds   6. has   7. I'll be working/I'm going to be working
II. 1. seems   2. sent   3. haven't received   4. is not functioning   5. are working   6. will start
III. 1. haven't seen   2. is at home recuperating   3. hurt   4. was playing   5. did she hurt   6. was trying   7. collided   8. fell   9. landed   10. twisted   11. has been wearing   12. hasn't been able   13. will not/won't be   14. Will her doctor allow/Is her doctor going to allow   15. will have had
IV. 1. Did you enjoy   2. I've never gone   3. had never gone   4. didn't know   5. were still trying   6. appeared   7. started   8. was singing   9. was
V. 1. grew up   2. greatly admired (possible: *had greatly admired*)   3. had become   4. became   5. contained   6. died   7. had been working   8. never finished   9. has become

1. has experienced	9. moves	17. sent
2. will experience	10. know	18. will...occur/is...going to occur
3. began	11. happened	19. have often helped
4. have occurred	12. struck	20. are studying
5. causes	13. were sitting	21. also appear
6. have developed	14. suddenly found	22. have developed
7. waves	15. died	23. will give
8. hold/are holding	16. collapsed	24. strikes

◇ PRACTICE TEST B, p. 41: *Verb tenses.*

1. A	6. A	11. D	16. D
2. A	7. B	12. A	17. C
3. B	8. B	13. A	18. B
4. C	9. C	14. A	19. A
5. C	10. B	15. D	20. D

Chapter 2: MODAL AUXILIARIES AND SIMILAR EXPRESSIONS

◇ PRACTICE 4, p. 45: *Imperatives.*

4. (Please) pass   5. Wake   6. Don't touch   7. Get   8. (Please) listen   9. (Please) read/study   10. Take   11. (Please) close/open   12. (Please) don't shout   13. Taste/Try   14. Meet   15. Help   16. (Please) turn/put   17. (Please) buy   18. Think   19. (Please) remember   20. (Please) be

◇ PRACTICE 5, p. 45: *Making polite requests.*

2. I see your (driver's) license   3. you give me a lift/ride   4. you check them/(take a) look at them   5. ...changing/if we changed our appointment   6. you give me directions/draw a map for me   7. I help you...you show me some slacks/I see some slacks   8. if we moved/ moving to different   9. I call you   10. you please turn off the TV...you turn it down/lower the volume

◇ PRACTICE 6, p. 46: *Making polite requests.*

Assign pair work. You may not want every pair of students to work on every item. Give each pair one or two items to prepare in a time limit of 5-8 minutes. Allow each group to "perform" its best dialogue for the other students. Then everyone can discuss reasons why some dialogues were more effective than others.

This exercise could also be assigned as written homework.

◇ PRACTICES 9 & 10, pp. 49–50. Should, ought to, had better.

Practice 9 could be used for small-group discussion. Practice 10 could be used for pair-work writing. [Answers depend on students' ideas.]

◇ PRACTICE 11, p. 50: *The past form of* should.

In pairs or small groups, students can discuss their opinions about each situation. One person in each group can record their answers. Then another person can read the answers to the whole class. You should probably set a time limit for the group work (about 3–5 minutes per item) and another for each person's report (one minute).

To save time, you may want to assign only one or two items to each small group. When they report their answers, students from other groups can discuss them and add their own ideas. You should probably set a time limit for the group work and discussions.

At the end of the exercise, the class can vote to choose the best answer or the most thoughtful group.

◇ PRACTICE 12, p. 51:   Be to.

You might make this a creative project. Students could produce a colorful poster for the school or classroom bulletin board, printing their list of rules on it carefully and clearly. Perhaps you could give them a different topic for their rules, such as use of the library, preparation of written homework, or care of equipment.

◇ PRACTICE 13, p. 52:   *Necessity, advisability, and expectations.*

The students need to use their imaginations in this exercise; most of them probably haven't had any experience in the roles described in the given situations. You could suggest other, more familiar roles of authority (e.g., the teacher of this class), or the students could invent their own authority roles. Perhaps they could write the answers for one of the given situations and also write answers for a situation of their own devising.

Take a few minutes to discuss item #1 with the whole class. Have them add other answers, using all the rest of the modals and similar expressions in the list.

This exercise is intended as written homework but can be used for group discussion or pair work.

◇ PRACTICE 14, p. 52:   Let's, why don't, shall I/we.

Item notes and possible completions:
1. ["sushi" = Japanese appetizers, small snacks]
2. we go down to the coffee house/we go to a movie . . . shall we go/leave
3. we look in the suburbs . . . Let's start with the North Side . . . we get a newspaper?
4. [Depend on students' ideas.]
5. get out of town . . . we go camping? . . . stay in a motel/an inn
6. [Depend on students' ideas.]
7. [Depend on students' ideas.]
8. panic/leap to conclusions/get upset over nothing/make a mountain out of a molehill . . . you call/phone her house/apartment/room? . . . you just relax/take it easy?
9. you try/have some? . . . go . . . I call/signal/get the waiter?

◇ PRACTICE 15, p. 54:   *Using* could *and* should *to make suggestions.*

[Depend on students' ideas.]

◇ PRACTICE 17, p. 55:   *Degrees of certainty:* must *and* may/might/could.

Students should discuss their choices and their reasoning process.
1. A [fairly certain; logical conclusion]
2. B [uncertain]
3. C [definite]
4. B [uncertain]
5. A [fairly certain; logical conclusion]
6. C [definite]
7. B [uncertain]
8. B [uncertain]
9. C [definite]
10. C [definite]

◇ **PRACTICE 18, p. 56:** *Making conclusions:* must *and* must not.

Students should discuss their reasons for their "best guesses."
Possible responses:
3. He must have seen this movie already.
4. She must have been tired. / She must be asleep.
5. She must not have heard them.
6. The fish must have been spoiled/bad/must not have been fresh.
7. Jeremy must like classical music.
8. Jeremy's wife must not like classical music/must like a different kind of music.
9. She must not have paid her telephone bill.
10. There must be a fire nearby.
11. She must have been to Paris.
12. The mushrooms must have been poisonous.

◇ **PRACTICE 19, p. 57:** *Degrees of certainty:* must.

Encourage the students to make between five and ten observations and "best guesses" about their immediate environment (i.e., where they are when they are writing these sentences). Tell them to observe anything a little unusual and then play the role of a detective.

Later, in class discussion, a student can present one of her/his observations and the rest of the class can try to figure out what "best guess" s/he made. For example:
STUDENT A: *There was a broken egg shell in the waste can.*
REST OF CLASS: *Who do you live with? Does he/she usually eat an egg for breakfast? Did you eat an egg for breakfast this morning? What time did you see the broken egg shell?* [And so on, until they can figure out the same conclusion that Student A made, that A's roommate must have had an egg for breakfast.]

◇ **PRACTICE 22, p. 60:** *Forms of modals.*

1. might be taking   2. must have been watching...must have forgot(ten)   3. should have bought...shouldn't have waited   4. must have been driving   5. must not have planned
6. must have been daydreaming...should have been paying...shouldn't have been staring
7. may have borrowed...couldn't have borrowed   8. must not have been listening
9. couldn't have told   10. must not have...must have been/must be sleeping   11. must be making/must make   12. must have left   13. should have taken...must be walking...might have decided...could be working/could work...may have called.

◇ **PRACTICE 23, p. 61:** *Degrees of certainty.*

Encourage the class to actually go to a public place (though they can, of course, visit that place in their imaginations to complete the assignment). Perhaps the whole class could go together to a zoo or public square.

As an alternative, show a video tape to the class. You could turn off the sound and have the class guess what the people on the tape are talking about and doing. Or you could show several minutes from the middle of a movie or TV show and have the students guess about the characters and the story.

As another alternative, you could supply pictures for the students to write about, perhaps news photos or posters depicting people and activities. It can be fun for you to supply snapshots of your family and friends for the students to make guesses about.

◇ **PRACTICE 25, p. 62:** Used to *and* be used to.

1. used to play   2. am used to driving   3. used to rely   4. am not used to standing
5. used to come   6. used to think   7. used to like   8. am used to taking   9. are used to commuting   10. used to travel

PRACTICE 27, p. 64: Would rather.

Students should be alert to signals for the present and past verbs. Item #1, for example, requires the past form of the modal (modal + *have* + past participle). [Answers depend on students' ideas.]

PRACTICE 29, p. 65: *Modals: dialogues.*

Students might work in pairs to complete the dialogues, with one student completing A's sentences and the other completing B's. The completed dialogues can be performed, discussed by the whole class, and/or written out and handed in. (See the INTRODUCTION, p. xv–xvi, for suggestions for using completion exercises.)

PRACTICE 30, p. 67: *Modals: dialogues.*

Assign only one dialogue to each pair. Some students may want to choose their own situations for dialogue construction. Have the pairs perform their dialogues with or without their "scripts."

PRACTICE 31, p. 68: *Discussion using modals.*

You may need to set a time limit for these discussions. Sometimes students get rather excited about the topics and don't want to stop! To conclude the exercise, you might ask the students to rewrite or expand on a sentence as given in the textbook so that all members of the group agree with the idea. The given ideas are, for the most part, overstated generalizations of opinion that need to be qualified, explained, and supported.

If these topics are unfamiliar or uncomfortable for your students, you might add some others that are closer to their immediate interests. Topics about their school, sports, clothing fashions, etc., may be productive.

These topics can also be used for writing.

PRACTICE 32, p. 68: *General review of verb forms.*

This entire exercise is a dialogue between two people, so you could choose two good speakers to read it. The other students should listen carefully and offer corrections or alternative answers, if appropriate.

1. had
2. happened
3. was driving
4. broke
5. did you do
6. pulled
7. got
8. started
9. shouldn't have done
10. should have stayed
11. are probably
12. started
13. had been walking/(had) walked
14. went
15. discovered
16. didn't have (BrE: hadn't)
17. can think
18. could/might have gone
19. could/might have tried
20. could/might have asked
21. asked
22. told
23. was
24. allowed
25. drove
26. must have felt
27. took
28. took
29. might get
30. will know
31. have to/have got to/had better/am going to leave
32. have to/have got to/am supposed to be
33. May/Can/Could I use
34. need
35. don't have/have no
36. I'll take

PRACTICE 33, p. 69: *Review of modals.*

A "short paragraph" is usually about five to eight sentences in length. You might want to set a limit for your students.

In marking their papers, focus on modals and verb tenses. Reward them for correct uses of these forms.

◇ PRACTICE TEST B, p. 71: *Modals and similar expressions.*

1. A	**6.** C	**11.** D	**16.** A
2. B	**7.** A	**12.** C	**17.** B
3. A	**8.** B	**13.** A	**18.** D
4. C	**9.** C	**14.** B	**19.** C
5. D	**10.** C	**15.** C	**20.** A

Chapter 3: The Passive

◇ PRACTICE 2, p. 75: *Forming the passive.*

This exercise provides a review of interrogative, negative, and affirmative forms in passive voice. It requires simple transformation. It can be used as an oral exercise in class, or if written, students can correct each other's answers.

1. a. Is your house being painted by Mr. Brown?
   b. No, it isn't being painted by him.
   c. It's being painted by my uncle.
2. a. Will the dishes be washed by Steve?
   b. No, they won't be washed by him.
   c. They'll be washed by the children.
3. a. Has the meeting been planned by Sue?
   b. No, it hasn't been planned by her.
   c. It has been planned by the committee.
4. a. Is that violin played by Mr. Parr?
   b. No, it isn't played by him.
   c. It is played by his son.
5. a. Are the books going to be returned to the library by Jack?
   b. No, they aren't going to be returned by him.
   c. They're going to be returned by his sister.
6. a. Was the ancient skeleton discovered by the archeologists?
   b. No, it wasn't discovered by them.
   c. It was discovered by a farmer.
7. a. Was the food being prepared by Sally?
   b. No, it wasn't being prepared by her.
   c. It was being prepared by her mother.
8. a. Will the letters have been typed by Ms. Anderson?
   b. No, they won't have been typed by her.
   c. They will have been typed by the secretary.

◇ PRACTICE 8, p. 80: *Using the "by phrase."*

3. Jack is being considered for that job.
4. The Mediterranean Sea is surrounded by three continents.
5. I got upset when I was interrupted in the middle of my story.
6. . . . he was embraced by each of his relatives.
7. Rome wasn't built in a day. [This is a famous saying. It means that we shouldn't expect to complete something both quickly and well. Good things take time to do well.]
8. Where is that information filed? [*They* is impersonal in the active sentence.]
9. . . . the dog had been chained to . . .
10. Were you annoyed (last night) by the noise from the neighbor's apartment (last night)?
11. . . . the news was broadcast all over the world.
12. Are those tractors made in this country, or are they imported?
13. . . . I was approached by a nice . . . .
14. Pencils will not be provided at the test, so . . . .

◇ PRACTICE 11, p. 82: *Active and passive.*

1. have complained . . . has been done [*to date* = until now]   **2.** went . . . had piled . . . had been shoved   **3.** are intimidated . . . buy   **4.** put . . . sold . . . was bought . . . was/had been looking . . . had already been sold   **5.** was invented . . . has assisted   **6.** brought . . . sent . . .

were asked . . . was discovered . . . is still called **7.** was recognized . . . was asked . . . took
8. occurred . . . were crossing . . . were swept . . . left . . . were found . . . were/had been seriously
injured . . . took

◇ **PRACTICE 13, p. 85:** *Present participle vs. past participle.*

3. equipped **4.** destroyed **5.** rubbing **6.** whispering **7.** erased **8.** performed
9. predicting **10.** vaccinated **11.** rehearsing **12.** billed [= The dentist will send him a
bill.]

◇ **PRACTICE 16, p. 87:** *Passive modals.*

2. been won **3.** scrub **4.** been vaccinated **5.** be taught **6.** replied **7.** been
stopped **8.** be revised **9.** trade **10.** participate **11.** be established **12.** eat
13. be distinguished **14.** be killed

◇ **PRACTICE 18, p. 90:** *Stative passive.*

1. is located **2.** are summarized **3.** is . . . listed **4.** is forbidden **5.** am . . .
acquainted **6.** is scheduled **7.** is overdrawn **8.** is cancel(l)ed [*canceled* = American;
cancelled = British] **9.** is wrinkled [*iron* = press] **10.** are equipped [*automobile* = American;
motor car = British] [Air bags are protective devices that inflate upon hard impact.] **11.** is
made **12.** is clogged

◇ **PRACTICE 21, p. 92:** *Present vs. past participles.*

3. known for **4.** provided with **5.** laughing **6.** satisfied with **7.** connected to
8. crossing **9.** involved in **10.** composed of **11.** accompanying **12.** blessed with
13. limited to **14.** annoyed at/with **15.** blowing

◇ **PRACTICE 23, p. 94:** *The passive with* get.

2. get accepted **3.** got cheated **4.** got fired **5.** got mugged [*to mug* = to rob; *scruffy* =
unkempt, dirty] **6.** get invited **7.** get dressed **8.** got caught **9.** got elected **10.** get
electrocuted **11.** got ruined **12.** got embarrassed

◇ **PRACTICE 26, p. 97:** *Participial adjectives.*

1. printing **2.** Experienced **3.** intended **4.** amusing **5.** manufactured
6. relaxing **7.** amazing **8.** expected **9.** approaching **10.** inquiring
11. visiting . . . winning . . . disappointed **12.** encouraging **13.** invigorating
14. contaminated

◇ **PRACTICE 27, p. 98:** *Verb form review, active and passive.*

3. are lost **4.** received **5.** are given **6.** are discriminated . . . have been enacted
7. had been offered **8.** finish [time clause] **9.** are returned [time clause] . . . will be given
10. have been destroyed **11.** were allowed **12.** was not fooled **13.** established . . . be
followed **14.** irritating . . . will be replaced **15.** was built . . . has often been described . . . was
designed . . . took **16.** is being/will be/is going to be judged . . . will be/are going to be
announced **17.** vending . . . kicked . . . fell . . . was seriously injured . . . ended . . . is still
wearing . . . vending [In fact, in the decade of the 1980s, eight people in the United States were
reported to have died from a vending machine falling on them.] **18.** proposed . . . is not being
offered [also: is not/will not be/is not going to be offered] **19.** jogged / has been jogging . . .
plans/is planning **20.** is conducted . . . are sent . . . are asked . . . is collected . . . is
published . . . use

◇ PRACTICE 29, p. 101:   *Writing.*

You might want to set a limit on the length of these compositions—say, 10–15 sentences. Expect that your students would have some difficulty in trying to translate explanations from another language into English; tell them to use only English reference books. If your students don't have access to reference books, perhaps they could interview a local expert, parent, or acquaintance about how some common object is made.

Another possibility is for you to invite an expert such as a ceramicist, weaver, or carpenter to speak to the class. The students can take notes as the basis for their compositions.

Another alternative is for you to photocopy a description of a process. First, discuss the process and analyze with the class the use of the passive in the passage. Then tell the students to put the passage aside and describe the process in their own words in writing.

Discuss the organization of the sample composition. It has an introduction (that announces the subject) leading to a thesis sentence ("Paper can be made . . . process."). The second paragraph discusses one topic: the mechanical process. The third paragraph is about the chemical process. The last paragraph concludes the process. The description of the process itself is in chronological order.

You may choose to ask the students to underline every example of a passive in their papers after they have finished writing and revising them. This helps you in marking their successes and errors. It also helps the students check their own use of the passive. Another possibility is for the students to read each other's compositions and underline each instance of the passive.

You might assign the first of these topics for homework and use the second one later as an in-class writing test.

◇ PRACTICE TEST B, p. 103:   *The passive.*

1. C	6. A	11. D	16. A
2. B	7. B	12. A	17. C
3. A	8. A	13. C	18. C
4. B	9. C	14. A	19. A
5. B	10. C	15. C	20. D

CHAPTER 4: Gerunds and Infinitives

◇ PRACTICE 2, p. 106:   *Gerunds as objects of prepositions.*

Students might need to consult Appendix 2 (Preposition Combinations) in the main book. Possible answers: [Depend on students' ideas.]

2. . . . for collecting dues.
3. . . . to working more than 40 hours a week.
4. . . . for being late.
5. . . . of winning a lot of money.
6. . . . to getting low marks on my tests.
7. . . . from going to the soccer match.
8. . . . in cleaning up the school yard.
9. . . . from entering this area.
10. . . . about attending the new school.
11. . . . for bringing me a newspaper.
12. . . . to hiring children.
13. . . . about having to do too much homework on weekends.

◇ PRACTICE 3, p. 106:   *Verbs followed by gerunds.*

[Answers depend on students' ideas.] Note these items in particular:
5. . . . mind having to stay . . . .   6. . . . consider going swimming . . . .   8. . . . discuss going shopping . . . .   9. . . . mention having to go . . . .   13. . . . quit worrying about . . . .

◇ PRACTICE 6, p. 109:   *Verbs followed by infinitives.*

    2. Laura reminded her roommate to set her alarm . . . .
    3. Mrs. Jones allowed each of the children to have . . . .
    4. The doctor advised my father to limit his sugar consumption.
    5. My parents often encouraged me to be independent.
    6. The children were warned not to swim . . . .
    7. The police officer ordered the reckless driver to pull over.
    8. Rose invited Gerald to come to her house Sunday . . . her parents.

◇ PRACTICE 8, p. 110:   *Gerund vs. infinitive.*

[Answers depend on students' creativity.]
1. remind someone to finish   **2.** postpone giving   **3.** be required to have   **4.** advise taking/advise someone to take   **5.** try to learn [less likely but also possible: *try learning*]
6. warn someone not to open   **7.** like going camping/like to go camping [*go to camp*: "camp" = a noun]   **8.** invite someone to go   **9.** promise not to tell/promise someone not to tell
10. not be permitted to take   **11.** ask someone to tell   **12.** begin blowing/begin to blow
13. remember calling/remember to call [with different meanings]   **14.** tell someone to wash
15. be told to be   **16.** avoid getting

◇ PRACTICE 13, p. 115:   *Gerund vs. infinitive.*

[Answers depend on students' ideas.]
1. playing   **2.** someone to save   **3.** telling   **4.** to get   **5.** someone to take   **6.** staying
7. someone not to buy   **8.** giving   **9.** going   **10.** travel(l)ing   **11.** taking
12. someone to go swimming   **13.** being   **14.** hearing   **15.** to tell   **16.** being
17. eating   **18.** to know   **19.** to get   **20.** saying   **21.** seeing   **22.** (someone) to give
23. to hire someone to work   **24.** to tell someone to be/telling someone to be [with different meanings]   **25.** someone to practice speaking   **26.** someone to keep trying to call

◇ PRACTICE 14, p. 115:   *Using gerunds as subjects.*

[Answers depend on students' creativity.]

◇ PRACTICE 15, p. 116:   *Using* it *+ infinitive.*

[Answers depend on students' creativity.]

◇ PRACTICE 17, p. 117:   *Adjectives followed by infinitives.*

Students can work in small groups, perhaps considering only three or four items. You might ask the students to use as many different expressions in the list as they can for each item. The group could then "vote" for the completion they like best, and the leader could present it to the rest of the class. [Answers depend on students' creativity.]

◇ PRACTICE 25, p. 123:   *Gerunds and infinitives.*

You could ask for two or three responses to each item. Or as a special challenge, you could set a limit on the number of words in each response; for example, not fewer than eight words nor more than twelve, or exactly ten words. Another possibility is for the students to draw a card on which a number is written from a stack you have prepared, or perhaps roll three dice, and then add that exact number of words to the sentence. Making the exercise into a game can be fun and involving for the students. Another benefit is that students understand that they can shorten (by eliminating nonessential words), lengthen (by combining ideas into compound and complex structures), and otherwise manipulate sentences as needed when revising their own writing. [Answers depend on students' creativity.]

◇ **PRACTICE 27, p. 124:** *Using verbs of perception.*

> Ask two or three students to write their sentences for one item on the chalkboard. Invite discussion from the class to decide which sentence they prefer and for what reasons.
>
> Or you could copy several good students' answers for each item and give them to each student in the class. Then you can lead a discussion of why those sentences are effective. [Answers depend on students' creativity.]

◇ **PRACTICE 29, p. 125:** *Let, help,* and causative verbs.

> [Answers depend on students' creativity.]

◇ **PRACTICE 30, p. 125:** *Special expressions followed by the* -ing *form of a verb.*

> [Answers depend on students' creativity.]
> **1.** remembering   **2.** waiting   **3.** learning   **4.** thinking [also possible: *(in order) to think*]
> **5.** playing   **6.** dreaming [also possible: *(in order) to dream*]   **7.** saying   **8.** singing and dancing   **9.** to study (with)   **10.** chatting   **11.** trying   **12.** taking

◇ **PRACTICE 33, p. 129:** *Verb form review.*

> **1.** to have . . . built . . . to do   **2.** watch . . . practice . . . finding   **3.** getting/being accepted . . . concentrating   **4.** hearing . . . play . . . forgetting . . . making . . . to relax . . . enjoy   **5.** to persuade . . . to give . . . to cut . . . working . . . to retire . . . take [Parallel infinitives: *to* is usually not repeated.] . . . being dedicated   **6.** wasting . . . to fail . . . doing   **7.** to commute . . . moving . . . to give . . . to live . . . be [parallel infinitives] . . . doing . . . doing   **8.** feel . . . to get . . . feeling . . . sneezing . . . coughing . . . to ask . . . to see . . . go   **9.** chewing . . . grabbing, holding, or tearing . . . swallow   **10.** Attending . . . embarrassing . . . to hide . . . get [parallel infinitives] . . . leave   **11.** recalling . . . being chosen . . . looking . . . laughing . . . acting . . . playing . . . being . . . achieving   **12.** to get . . . running . . . having . . . sprayed   **13.** being treated . . . threatening to stop working . . . to listen   **14.** cleaning/to be cleaned . . . sweeping/to be swept . . . washing/to be washed . . . dusting/to be dusted . . . Reading . . . doing   **15.** being . . . being . . . to be understood . . . to bridge . . . teaching   **16.** having been given . . . forming . . . to accept . . . going . . . being . . . having been exposed   **17.** Finding . . . to be . . . being exposed . . . staying . . . to avoid . . . to minimize . . . getting . . . to get . . . eat [parallel infinitives] . . . taking . . . to prevent catching   **18.** being inconvenienced or hurt [parallel passive gerunds] . . . to remind . . . to remove . . . to turn . . . to buckle ["buckle up"=connect one's seat belt] . . . to shut . . . to fill . . . to forget to do . . . driving . . . (to) avoid making . . . being instructed . . . to perform . . . being reminded to carry

◇ **PRACTICE 35, p. 133:** *Verb forms.*

> Encourage the students to use a personal experience in the introductory paragraph. You might want to set a limit (350 to 500 words). If you want a shorter composition, assign only a personal experience the writer has had that is related to one of the topics.
>
> When marking the papers, focus on verb forms. Point out good usage as well as errors. Perhaps excerpt sentences or passages to be reproduced for class discussion.

◇ **PRACTICE TEST B, p. 135:** *Gerunds and infinitives.*

1. D	**6.** C	**11.** D	**16.** C
2. D	**7.** C	**12.** A	**17.** D
3. A	**8.** C	**13.** B	**18.** C
4. B	**9.** B	**14.** D	**19.** A
5. B	**10.** A	**15.** A	**20.** D

Appendix 1: SUPPLEMENTARY GRAMMAR UNITS

◇ **PRACTICE 10, p. 141:** *Nouns, verbs, adjectives, adverbs, prepositions.*

This exercise can be used in class discussion to make sure that the students understand the basic terminology used in the textbook. The exercise can be expanded by asking them to identify words in addition to those that are underlined. The material can also be used to discuss sentence structure; you could focus on the elements of a simple sentence or preview the compound-complex structures covered in Chapters 6–9. (Some teachers like to diagram sentences for their students.) In addition, you could ask the class to discuss punctuation and capitalization.

2. whales = NOUN ... mammals = NOUN ... breathe = VERB [Point out the spelling and pronunciation of *breathe* (verb) and *breath* (noun).] ... air = NOUN [Note that in this sentence *live* is an adjective and *young* is a noun. You might ask students to find these particular uses of these two words in their dictionaries. Mention that it can be helpful to determine the grammatical function of a word in order to know which definition to look at in a dictionary.]
3. highly = ADVERB ... trainable = ADJECTIVE ... intelligent, sensitive = ADJECTIVES ... refused = VERB ... Finally = ADVERB ... immediately = ADVERB ... took, shared = VERBS
4. dive = VERB ... deeply = ADVERB ... beneath = PREPOSITION ... surface = NOUN ... under = PREPOSITION ... water = NOUN ... for = PREPOSITION
5. migrations = NOUN ... among = PREPOSITION ... swim = VERB ... from = PREPOSITION ... to = PREPOSITION ... icy = ADJECTIVE
6. with = PREPOSITION ... wide = ADJECTIVE ... clicks, whistles, songs = NOUNS ... gather = VERB ... around = PREPOSITION ... communicate = VERB ... through = PREPOSITION

◇ **PRACTICE 17, p. 148:** *Information questions.*

Practice 17 is a transformation exercise whose purpose is to review question words and forms. The questions the students make should produce the words in parentheses as short answers. Student A could ask the question, and Student B could say the short answer.

As an expansion of the exercise, the class could provide other possible answers to the questions. For example, in item #1:

A: *How do you take your coffee?*
B: *Black.* OR *With milk.* OR *With cream and sugar.*

2. What kind of dictionary do you have? [have you?/have you got?] [Answer: English-English. OR Bilingual. OR Spanish-English, etc.]
3. What does he do for a living? [Answer: Runs a grocery store, etc.]
4. Who was Margaret talking to?/To whom was Margaret talking? [Answer: Her uncle, etc.]
5. How many people showed up for the meeting?
6. Why could none of the planes take off?
7. What was she thinking about?/About what was she thinking?
8. How fast/How many miles per hour [OR an hour] were you driving when the policeman stopped you? [Point out that the subject-verb inversion occurs in the main clause, not the dependent (adverbial) clause.]
9. What kind of food do you like best?
10. Which apartment is yours?/Where is your apartment?
11. What is Oscar like? [Possibly: What kind of person/man is Oscar?]
12. What does Oscar look like?
13. Whose book fell to the floor?
14. Why isn't Abby here?
15. When will all of the students in the class be informed of their final grades? [Point out that even when there is a long subject, only the first auxiliary precedes it. The rest of the verb follows the complete subject.]
16. How do you feel?
17. Which book did you prefer?
18. What kind of music do you like?

19. How late is the plane expected to be?
20. Why did the driver of the stalled car light a flare?
21. Which pen do you want?
22. What's the weather like in July?
23. How do you like your steak?
24. How did you do on the test?
25. How many seconds are there in a year? [For fun, ask the students to figure out how many minutes (525,600) and hours (8760) there are in a year.]

◇ PRACTICE 18, p. 148: *Information questions.*

    Students can practice in pairs. If the exercise is used in class discussion, you should model spoken contractions for the students [e.g., "when're," "what color're," "what kind of tea's that," "what'd ya'"].
3. Who is/Who's that letter from?   **4.** Who wrote that letter?   **5.** Whose coat is that?
6. When are Alice and John going to get married?   **7.** Which/Whose team won?   **8.** What color are her eyes?   **9.** What color is her hair?   **10.** What kind of tea is that?   **11.** What do you usually drink with your breakfast?   **12.** How long does it usually take you to eat breakfast? [Less likely: *How many minutes . . .?*]   **13.** How did you get to the airport?   **14.** How many brothers and sisters do you have/have you?   **15.** Where did you grow up?   **16.** How long does it take to get there by plane?   **17.** What kind of novels/books do you like to read?
18. Which chapters/What/What chapters will the test cover? [*cover* = include, comprise]
19. Why did Frank quit school?/How come Frank quit school?   **20.** How long has she been sick?   **21.** How many (people) are you going to invite?   **22.** Which camera should I buy?
23. Who discovered radium?   **24.** What are you doing?   **25.** How is/How's everything going?

◇ PRACTICE 19, p. 149: *Information questions.*

    Students can make up questions in class discussion or write dialogues to hand in. If the exercise is written, have the students write both the question and the answer.
    Examples: **6:** How do you spell *sitting*?   **15.** Where are you from? Where is Saudi Arabia located? What is the population? What is the major religion? What is its principal product? What is the capital?

◇ PRACTICE 20, p. 150: *Asking questions.*

    [Answers depend on students' creativity.] In item #**4**, the interviewer (Speaker A) says: "Mr./Ms. _____, isn't it?" This means that the interviewer is identifying the other person with the name that is on the job application paper.

◇ PRACTICE 21, p. 150: *Shortened yes/no questions.*

    This can be done quickly as a group or class exercise. Two students can read the dialogue aloud from the book, then another student can give the complete form of the question that has been shortened.
1. *Do you* need some help?   **2.** *Are you* expecting someone?   **3.** *Did you* stay up late last night? [*Yup* = Yes (very informal)]   **4.** *Have you* ever been there before?   **5.** *Are you* nervous? [*Who me?* = (surprised) Are you talking about me? Do you think I'm nervous?]   **6.** *Do you* want a cup of coffee? [*Only if it's already made.* = Don't make a new pot of coffee just for me.]   **7.** *Have you* heard any news . . .?   **8.** A: *Are you* hungry? B: . . . Are you *hungry?*

If you ask students to write this exercise on paper for homework, they should underline the articles. This makes it easy for you to check.

If you do this exercise orally, it can be difficult for the students to hear the articles accurately. Try this technique: Give each student four cards or pieces of paper about 5″ (12.5 cm) square. On each card they should write one article (*a, an, the,* or *Ø*) in large letters. You should do the same. Then a student (or you) can read a sentence aloud. When the space for an article occurs, everybody holds up the card with the necessary article so that you can see it. Then you hold up the same word so the whole class can see it. Sometimes this creates a little confusion and laughter as students pick out their cards, but it keeps everyone actively involved in the lesson. Discuss any questions that arise.

1. . . . *a* teacher . . . *a* computer programmer . . . *an* architect . . . *an* apartment . . . *a* house.
2. . . . *the* name of *a* famous architect . . . *the* architect . . . *a* hotel in Tokyo . . . *The* hotel . . . *Ø* earthquakes.
3. . . . *a* sandy shore . . . *Ø* animals . . . *the* surface . . . *Ø* life . . . *Ø* crabs, *Ø* shrimp [*Shrimp* is plural here; it has the same form in both singular and plural, like *deer* or *sheep*.], *Ø* worms, *Ø* snails, and *Ø* other kinds of *Ø* marine animals
4. . . . *the* sand [of that beach] . . . *Ø* animals . . . *a* crab . . . *The* crab . . . *a* good time at *the* beach
5. . . . *Ø* stones, *Ø* glass, and *Ø* keys . . . *a* person
6. . . . *a* recent newspaper article . . . *an* Australian swimmer . . . *a* shark . . . *a* group . . . *the* shark . . . *the* swimmer, *the* dolphins . . . *the* swimmer's life
7. . . . *Ø* evidence . . . *Ø* dolphins . . . *Ø* nature . . . *an* average . . . *Ø* suicide
8. . . . *a* committee . . . *The* committee . . . *the* following proposals . . . *a* new sewage disposal plant . . . *a* new park . . . *the* present proposal, *the* new park . . . *a* swimming pool
9. . . . *the* southeast corner . . . *a* landmark . . . *a* bolt . . .
10. . . . *Ø* old cars . . . *a* 1922 automobile . . . *an* antique car
11. . . . *Ø* power windows . . . *a* cassette player . . . *a* multi-adjustable driver's seat
12. . . . *Ø* jokes . . . *a* frog . . . *a* lunchbox . . . *a* table . . . *the* school lunchroom [Other articles are possible. The given answers assume there is more than one table in a school lunchroom and that there's only one lunchroom in a school.]
13. *Ø* Most mirrors . . . *Ø* glass . . . *a* thin layer . . . *Ø* silver . . . *Ø* aluminum
14. . . . *the* sun . . . *the* hours . . . *A* person's . . . *Ø* cancer
15. *Ø* Phonograph records . . . *Ø* compact discs
16. . . . *a* coat hanger . . . *the* lock . . . *the* window . . . *the* driver's seat . . . *the* door . . . *the* police . . . *a* taxi . . . *the* car
17. . . . *a* fly . . . *the* ceiling . . . *the* fly . . . *the* last second . . . *the* ceiling
18. . . . *the* last sentence . . . *the* end